Comments on other *Amazing Stories* from readers & reviewers

"You might call them the non-fiction response to Harlequin romances: easy to consume and potentially addictive."
Robert Martin, *The Chronicle Herald*

"Tightly written volumes filled with lots of wit and humour about famous and infamous Canadians."
Eric Shackleton, *The Globe and Mail*

"This is popular history as it should be ... For this price, buy two and give one to a friend."
Terry Cook, a reader from Ottawa, on *Rebel Women*

"Stories are rich in description, and bristle with a clever, stylish realness."
Mark Weber, *Central Alberta Advisor*, on *Ghost Town Stories II*

"The resulting book is one readers will want to share with all the women in their lives."
Lynn Martel, *Rocky Mountain Outlook*, on *Women Explorers*

"[The books are] *long on plot and character and short on the sort of technical analysis that can be dreary for all but the most committed academic."*
Robert Martin, *The Chronicle Herald*

"A compelling read. Bertin ... has selected only the most intriguing tales, which she narrates with a wealth of detail."
Joyce Glasner, *New Brunswick Reader*, on *Strange Events*

"The heightened sense of drama and intrigue, combined with a good dose of human interest, is what sets Amazing Stories *apart."*
Pamela Klaffke, *Calgary Herald*

INCREDIBLE TALES
OF THE ROYAL
CANADIAN AIR FORCE

AMAZING STORIES®

INCREDIBLE TALES OF THE ROYAL CANADIAN AIR FORCE

Unsung Heroes of World War II

CYNTHIA J. FARYON

PUBLISHED BY ALTITUDE PUBLISHING CANADA LTD.
1500 Railway Avenue, Canmore, Alberta T1W 1P6
www.altitudepublishing.com
www.amazingstories.ca
1-800-957-6888

Extreme care has been taken to ensure that all information presented in
this book is accurate and up to date. Neither the author nor the
publisher can be held responsible for any errors.

Publisher	Stephen Hutchings
Series Editor	Diana Marshall
Editors	Gayl Veinotte and Laurie Drukier
Cover and layout	Zoe Howes

We acknowledge the financial support of the Government
of Canada through the Book Publishing Industry Development
Program (BPIDP) for our publishing activities.

Altitude GreenTree Program
Altitude Publishing will plant twice as many trees as were used
in the manufacturing of this product.

Library and Archives Canada Cataloguing in Publication

Faryon, Cynthia J., 1956-
   Incredible tales of the Royal Canadian Air Force / Cynthia J. Faryon.

(Amazing stories)
ISBN 1-55439-181-4

   1. World War, 1939-1945--Aerial operations, Canadian. 2. Canada. Royal
Canadian Air Force--History--World War, 1939-1945. 3. Canada. Royal Canadian
Air Force--Biography. I. Title. II. Series: Amazing stories (Canmore, Alta.)

D792.C2F36 2006   940.54'4971   C2006-905943-8

For general information on Altitude Publishing and the Amazing Stories, including all books published by
Altitude Publishing, please call our order line at 1-800-957-6888. For reseller information, including discounts
and premium sales, please call our sales department at 403-678-9592. For press review copies, author inter-
views, or other publicity information, please contact our marketing department at 403-283-7934, or via fax at
403-283-7917. For general information, visit our Web sites: *www.amazingstories.ca* and
www.altitudepublishing.com

Printed and bound in Canada by Friesens
2 4 6 8 9 7 5 3 1

To my grandchildren: Rebecca, Brandon, Courtenay,
Alex, Jacob, and Owen, so they, too, will remember …

Contents

Prologue
Silent Hero

As I sat fidgeting in a church pew on Sunday, November 11, 1984, I glanced curiously at the Legion uniforms around me. So many old geezers, I thought irreverently. Then I turned my attention to our minister, who was introducing our guest speaker in honour of Remembrance Day; it was a morning I will never forget.

Larry, a tall man in his 60s, came forward and shook the minister's hand. Taking his place at the podium, he began to address the congregation in a quiet voice. Although he appeared calm, his eyes shifted nervously over his audience, betraying his inner feelings. He told us how, as the oldest son of a northern Saskatchewan farmer, he had eagerly signed up with the Royal Canadian Air Force (RCAF) in June of 1941. After training in Brandon, Manitoba, he shipped out to England to fly with the Royal Air Force (RAF), along with many other Canadians. Due to keen marksmanship, Larry had been assigned to No. 77 Squadron as a rear gunner.

I found myself chuckling, along with the rest of the congregation, as Larry described the awkwardness of folding his tall frame into the tiny compartment that housed the rear guns on the Halifax bombers. Quietly, almost as an after-thought, he also stated that the life expectancy of a rear gunner during World War II was approximately five weeks. Yet, I knew from the introduction he had received from our minister that this brave man had flown 38 missions over three years.

In a voice punctuated with difficult emotions, he described his horror as another bomber in his squad was fatally hit by anti-aircraft artillery while flying a bombing mission over Germany. He recounted his desperate prayers that the pilot dump his load early, giving the plane a chance to limp back and bring the crew home safely. However, that day, Larry witnessed true heroism. The ill-fated bomber doggedly smoked its way to the designated bombing site and dropped its load on the target as planned, instead of on some unsuspecting civilian family. Larry and the rest of his crew watched helplessly; the plane disintegrated as the crew jumped from the wounded guts of the bomber — some with parachutes, some without. Larry watched in horror as enemy fighters gunned those suspended helplessly by their parachutes before they disappeared into the unknown.

Larry paused, reaching down to grasp a glass of water in his shaking hand. I noted the deafening silence of the congregation around me. Those in uniform sat in stony remembrance, while those of us born free of the horrors of war wrestled with the inherited memories of what this man had survived. I looked with compassion at Larry, disturbed to his soul by the horrors of war, and began to understand.

Prologue

Clearing his throat, Larry smiled apologetically before he continued. He then described a daylight mission he had flown that had brought him face to face with his own mortality. The purpose of each mission was to hit a predetermined target, he explained, some obscure point on a map. Larry, like many others on these assignments, tried not to think of the people this target represented. For, although he was fifth-generation Canadian, he was of Dutch-German descent. He tried not to wonder if he was bombing a cousin or if a relative was flying raids over London.

During this mission, German fighters attacked the bombers. Larry saw a Messerschmitt closing in fast. As the rear guns were the first targets when attacking a bomber, the German fighter had him in his sights. Larry's guns jammed, so he couldn't swing around to defend himself or his crew. Thinking it was all over, he stared in mortal fascination as death screamed at him in slow motion. He looked into the cockpit of the enemy plane, right into the eyes of the German pilot, and waited for the inevitable blast from the guns. The pilot seemed to hesitate as he looked back into Larry's eyes. The enemy lifted his hand in a half salute and was gone without firing a shot. Larry paused. Then he quietly said that he would like to meet that man someday. He would like to thank him for sparing his life, and the lives of his two sons, three daughters, and fourteen grandchildren.

Glancing at the medals he wore on his chest I recognized the prestigious Distinguished Flying Cross (DFC) and waited eagerly to hear how he'd earned it. I was to be disappointed. Larry never related his own acts of heroism. Instead, he spoke of the look of death he had seen on the faces of some flyers before each mission. He spoke of the unmistakable aura around those who would not make it back and the ultimate despair the survivors felt when the mission was complete and those marked had been lost behind enemy lines. He spoke of all who died as personal heroes, and I sensed he wasn't the only mourner present.

As I listened, my respect grew for the experiences of the proud people in uniforms, and I reflected on how my own life had been marked and shaped by the bravery performed while our world was at war. I thought of my father's active service: my childhood frustration of not being allowed to chew gum, or crunch potato chips or raw vegetables around him. My mother always explained it was due to the shell shock my dad had suffered during the war, but being a child I hadn't understood. I also remembered that my dad would have nightmares after watching a war movie before going to bed. I remembered with compassion the time my father had made a hasty retreat during a fireworks display. I can still see him wearing a haunted expression, pacing and chain-smoking. I'd known that all these episodes were the result of his wartime experiences, but I'd only understood it on the most superficial level.

In all the years I was growing up, I never heard my father talk about the war; not of any of his missions nor of his friends who had died. He kept his medals tucked away in a drawer, along with a picture of his squadron, marks drawn under all those who'd been killed in action. He chose to wear his scars silently; the scars that had helped shape my childhood. During that unforgettable Remembrance Day service on November 11, 1984, I listened as my father, Larry, chose to break his silence — I finally understood.

Four years later on a cold, bright autumn day, we buried my father, Flying Officer Lawrence G. Cramer, RCAF, DFC. As I looked sadly at the impersonal wood box adorned with pure white long-stemmed roses, I mourned all the riches my children and I had lost at his passing. How much I owed this man: my father, my childhood hero.

Chapter 1
Fire on the Tarmac

t is a balmy night, more like the first day of August instead of June 27, 1944, and relatively quiet. The large airfield at Tholthorpe, England, is home to No. 420 and No. 425 Squadrons. Halifax ground crews wait anxiously, as bombers (or "kites," "heavies," or "birds," as they are often called) are off attacking two V-1 rocket sites: one at Wizernès and one at Forêt D'Eawy in the Pas-de-Calais area.

Those aircrews not on tonight's rotation have turned in by now, albeit with one ear listening for the throaty throb of Hercules engines returning home to roost. No one on the base really sleeps until the planes return. A missing plane means a missing crew, empty chairs in the mess, and the dreaded initials next to the names: POW (prisoner of war), MIA (missing in action), or worse, KIA (killed in action). And those on duty try to resign themselves to the inevitable: some may not return. That means the empty bunk will be cleaned out, letters will be written to loved ones back home, and a new fresh-faced kid will take his place — another crew member to get to know and care about and, eventually, to worry about or mourn for.

On duty tonight is Squadron Leader Ken Running, from Smiths Falls, Ontario. He was a first-year student in aviation medicine when he enlisted and is now serving as senior medical officer at Tholthorpe.

Ken is wide-awake. As a medical officer, he knows every man on the base. He has given them medical exams and listened to their fears and nightmares. He is bound by the Hippocratic Oath and patient confidentiality; the men know they can trust him. He has seen them naked and given them vaccinations, even picking up a few of the toughest ones off the floor when they fainted from the sight of needles. They are closer than friends, and in the mess hall or the local pub, they open up to him. He knows which ones he should recommend for leave, whom to ground for a while, and who is best fit to fly. So when a crew doesn't make it home, he feels responsible and questions whether he missed a sign.

Ken sighs as he paces in the control tower. Something is up; he can feel the hair bristling on the back of his neck. From the look of the ground crew, acting like nervous fathers waiting for their sons to bring home the family car, he isn't the only anxious one.

Then, quietly on the night breeze, he hears it: a soft whir from far away. The first Halifax radios in: I'm coming in on three. While not the worst scenario, one down engine reduces the heavy's ability to manoeuvre and may also mean other damage to the plane the pilot isn't aware of. Emergency crews scramble — ambulances and a pumper truck are standing by on the tarmac.

"He's an experienced pilot," Ken mutters to himself as he jumps into the passenger side of one of the ambulances. He rolls down the window and rapes the air with his eyes for the first glimpse of the kite in trouble. White knuckles grip the door handle when suddenly he sees it: a smudge in the sky that blocks the stars as they fade into morning.

Ken can hear the throaty whir turn into a deep throbbing as the plane approaches. He swears he hears the fourth engine sputter as the Halifax circles, swings wide, and shoots for the airstrip with wheels extended like the talons of an eagle. The ground crews hold their breath. There's silence but for the high whine of engines, the screeching of tires, and a rumble of rubber on tarmac. The Halifax slows, the men on the ground sigh, and smiles appear.

One down …

Two more kites are spotted on the lightening horizon. There's smoke billowing from one. The night isn't over yet. A Halifax limps over the airstrip on two engines, fully loaded with 13,000 pounds of TNT still in its belly. Fuel is falling from one wing and he can't do a wide swing out. The bomber tilts at a dangerous angle. The emergency trucks rev their engines; the fire truck is already shooting out to the landing strip, and the sand truck is standing by to dry up the fuel on the runway. The bomber hits the tarmac and bounces as the wheels squeal on the ground. Sparks fly and everyone prays they don't ignite the fuel. Seconds later they're down; the crew pours out of the hatch below the cockpit, and the fire truck hoses the gas off the runway so the next bomber can land. The broken bird is towed to dispersal to be unloaded; holes from shrapnel and flak dot its length. The ground crew have their work cut out for them to make it ready to fly again.

"Better them than me," the medical officer mutters to himself.

The third kite circles, swings wide, and hits the tarmac as if all four engines are purring. All but one are home safely. After an anxious delay, the last Halifax radios in. They, too, are coming in on three engines. Sergeant M. Lavoie from No. 425 Squadron is flying the Halifax III MZ-683. He and his crew successfully bombed the target of Forêt D'Eawy, but were hit in one engine by anti-aircraft fire. Approaching the landing strip at Tholthorpe, the wireless operator lets the ground know they have one engine out.

The pilot checks with the flight engineer on the levels of fuel in the active tank and instructs him to disengage the undercarriage up-locks and secure the clips. The engineer checks with the pilot that the flaps lever is in the neutral position and turns the isolating cock half a turn. The flaps are dropping and the engineer regulates their descent with the cock.

At this point, the pilot should be reducing his speed to 241 kilometres per hour and lowering flaps 30 to 40 degrees, reducing his speed further to 140 while lowering the undercarriage. It's a touchy landing with a strong cross wind and only three engines. The manoeuvrability of the bomber has been compromised, so the pilot decides to keep the speed up a little high. The Halifax comes in too fast and overshoots. Realizing his error, the pilot brakes too quickly once he's on the runway, and swings wide, crashing into another Halifax (LW-680 KW-U) waiting at dispersal. In a domino effect, this bomber, fully loaded with bombs, hits yet another parked Halifax (MZ-618 KW-J), which has also recently returned from Forêt D'Eawy. All three aircraft burst into flames and Lavoie's crew are trapped inside the crippled bomber; the pilot is unconscious, slumped over in the cockpit, helpless.

Seeing the bomber swing wide and hit the fully loaded Halifax, Ken Running yells at his staff, "Get those men out!"

Ken jumps from the ambulance while it's still moving to help rescue the trapped and injured crew members. He and his staff, other air and ground crew, start beating the flames back to access the hatches. Fire extinguishers whoosh into the black smoke and flames that shoot high into the air. The hatches are pried open and the men work to extract the aircrew and fight through the fire to reach the injured pilot. He seems unreachable as the heat from the flames builds to a dangerous intensity, scorching the would-be rescuers. Seeing no other way into the bomber, Ken wraps his arms with his jacket and enters the burning wreckage through a gaping hole in the side of the fuselage. Flipping the flight jacket off his arms once inside, he drapes it over his head as he battles through the fire to the cockpit. He coughs from the smoke, and the heat burns his lungs with every breath. Flames scorch his boots and singe his pants and shirt. He can feel the cloth hot against his skin and wonders how long he has before he's engulfed in the fire. The pilot is coming to and calling weakly for help. He's trapped in his seat, still in his harness. The smoke has overwhelmed him and he's dazed, but conscious enough to know he's in danger of being burned alive where he sits. Ken stumbles through the black smoke and reaches the cockpit. With the help of another rescuer, the two manage to release the clasp on the pilot's harness. The rest of the plane is too hot and too far-gone for them to drag the pilot back through the body of the plane. The escape hatch below them is still jammed shut. Ken is only too aware of the fuel left in the tanks. Once the flames reach it, there will be no getting out alive. The only chance for escape is through the front of the plane.

The two men kick out the front Plexiglas of the windshield. Ken lifts the pilot from under his arms and hoists him through the windshield to waiting arms below. Then, he and his helper leap through the window. Ken yells for everyone to clear out, "She's going to blow!" People scatter in all directions. Injured crew members are half carried, half dragged toward safety when suddenly a ten-cwt bomb from the aircraft behind them at dispersal explodes with a mighty shock wave, throwing everyone to the ground and sending a column of flames and debris high into the air. A piece of shrapnel whizzes through the air and hits Air Commodore A. Ross, severing his arm below the elbow. Blood pours onto the ground as goes into shock. Ken, singed, bruised, and bleeding from minor cuts, wraps a belt around the commodore's arm to stem the flow of blood. He orders two men nearby to take the man to sick bay where help is waiting.

Two other members of the ground crews, Leading Aircraftman MacKenzie and Leading Aircraftman Wolfe, are also injured. They, along with the injured aircrew, are evacuated to sick bay. It isn't enough for Ken to have rescued them once, now he has a full day's work ahead of him to save their lives a second time.

Before all are safely off the tarmac, another explosion sends shrapnel and flames in all directions. The air base fire crew works hard to put the flames out as black smoke billows high into the air.

Many hours later the fires are out. The area looks like a war zone. But the injured are looked after, and those in the worst condition are safely moved to the military hospital in York. They all recover.

Chapter 2
RCAF out in the Cold

t's cold and blustery on the Rock at 8 a.m. on a chilly November morning. Gander, Newfoundland, is a busy place: the air base is humming. Three men are about to take off for Britain in a Douglas A-20 Boston light twin-engine bomber. The pilot, David Harrison Goodlet, and Navigator Al Nash and Flight Sergeant and Wireless Air-gunner Arthur Weaver are transporting the bomber overseas for the RCAF.

For Flight Lieutenant Goodlet from Simcoe, Ontario, the flight is expected to be a piece of cake. David is serving with the No. 313 Ferry Training Unit and is considered one of the RCAF's finest instructors. Sitting in the cockpit of the light bomber, he's looking forward to the trip. Even though Newfoundland is a big place, and he's only been here a few

The Douglas A-20

weeks, he feels that nebulous sense of being cut off from the rest of Canada by the crashing Atlantic Ocean.

The bomber had left Dorval Airport in Montreal on October 31, 1942. After the routine technical stop in Gander, by November 10 they are ready to cross the Atlantic to Britain, stopping in Greenland for fuel.

The nice thing about the small twin-engine bomber is how easy it is to handle. Revving up the engines to that I-want-to-leave-the-earth whine, the wind from the props beats the air. As the plane rolls along the tarmac, the vibrations from the engines could probably rattle the fillings right out of the crew's teeth. Pilots live for the sensation.

David nods to the ground crew as the plane rolls past. Out of the parking bay at dispersal, David throttles back the left engine and opens the mixture slightly to the right. Using the rudder and brakes in succession, the small bird swings easily to the left. Soon, they are waiting on the runway for the green light.

"Good to go?" the pilot checks with the others.

"Good to go," they answer, almost in unison.

The light at the station hut flashes green. David opens the throttle steadily and smoothly to the correct boost. The bird gathers speed. Right before liftoff, David eases the control column forward to help the tail up into flying position and level with the ground. They are speeding forward, still bound by gravity, when suddenly the airstrip falls away below them and they're weightless. The clouds are white and fluffy, begging for someone to step out on them. It doesn't get much better than this.

All clear. David smiles; he's almost ready to relax. He adjusts the levers and hears a clunk below as the undercarriage is raised and locked into flying position.

The sun is up over the horizon and there is a slight mist over the ocean. Newfoundland is fading quickly into the background behind. Details merge as the island looks more and more like a rock surrounded by crashing waves.

Two hours out of Newfoundland, they hit a thick bank of fog over the Atlantic. David checks the instruments and adds carb heat to guard against icing. Everything else seems to be working fine so he isn't concerned, until Arthur says the radio's dead. Al can't take sun shots in the fog to check their location, so David adjusts the propellers to climbing pitch and opens the throttles to maximum boost, easing the control column back. Almost immediately the plane bucks and the engines sputter. David levels out for a moment and then tries again with the same result. He can't climb; the engines are so badly iced, they threaten to stall every time he tries to gain altitude. David turns up the carb heat full, but in this damp fog he starts to worry that the heat won't be enough to melt the ice starting to gather at an alarming rate. Worse news is that Al can't be sure they are still over the Atlantic; all he can be sure of is that somewhere out there, in all that thick, cold, damp fog, is Greenland — in November, one big glacier. And somewhere along the coast of the frozen chunk of rock are mountains.

David flies blind and does his best to hold steady at 4,572 metres. It's –26 degrees Celsius and the heater works continually. He wishes he could climb just a bit more to get their bearings. He has no idea where he's flying to, or what he's flying over. Arthur reports there is only about a half hour of fuel left. David has no choice but to descend and try to find a place to land. Without navigation, though, there is no way of knowing how far the nearest base is or how close that coastal mountain range is. Still, their best chance of survival is to land.

At 1,158 metres, they break out of the fog and find

themselves about 24 kilometres inland. To their left rise the jagged mountains David was so concerned about. None of them can see any sign of civilization, but directly below, the area looks good for landing. There are deep ice crevasses criss-crossing the glacier very close to the ocean, and David does a few circles to make sure he has the room to give the crevasses a wide berth. If the plane slides into one of those holes, they'll never be found.

Picking a spot to put down, David tells everyone to brace for a rough one. He decides to leave the landing gear up in case the terrain is too rugged or the deep snow grabs the wheels and flips the plane. As long as the snow is soft enough, the belly of the airplane should hold up and ride the surface of the glacier like a toboggan. If it's too deep, though, they could bury themselves.

Dropping the speed to 177 kilometres per hour, holding the nose up, David eases the plane down. The snow is so white against the grey day, it's hard to judge where the ground actually starts. As gently as possible, David descends and lands the bomber belly first. Snow flies in all directions but the flaps help to slow the bird down. When she finally settles, everyone breathes a sigh of relief. No one is hurt; the only damage are the props on one of the engines, the radio antennae, and a broken water bottle.

David decides to make use of the daylight while they still have it. Opening the hatch, he leaps to the ground and sinks to his hips in snow. Quickly, he reaches out for the plane to keep from sinking further. The other two grab him quickly, and laughing heartily at him, drag him back inside. The three shut the door firmly against the unfriendly elements and sit down to discuss their next step. Looking at one another, the reality of their situation finally hits them. Outside is the glacier, the ocean, and hundreds of kilometres to civilization. They are at war, the radio doesn't work, and they've drifted off course. No one will even know they are missing for hours, and when they do, where will they look?

Lighting up cigarettes, they sit silently for a few very long moments. Through the windows the daylight outside is turning a surreal rose colour. The only sure thing is that night is closing in. They're cold and on their own. If they are on Greenland, the night will be 17 hours long with an hour of dawn and one of twilight, and daylight will only last five hours. Besides the shortage of water, hypothermia is their next worst enemy — falling asleep means death. They agree to keep each other moving; if one drifts off, the others will wake him and get him onto his feet.

Silence closes in. They smoke, stare, and avoid each other's eyes.

Shaking himself out of the shocked silence, Dave gets up and checks the thermometer.

Minus 34.

Retrieving a flashlight, he tells the others to get ready for a long night. They need food, water, and something to help keep them warm.

Al digs out the meal they were issued for the flight. The sandwiches are frozen solid. Breaking off a small piece at a time, they thaw them out by sucking on them. Opening the thermos of coffee, they find it's also frozen. It's so solid there is no way of extracting it from the container. The only surviving water bottle is almost as frozen, but they manage to drink a small amount each, leaving an unreachable lump of ice in the bottom of the jug. Al shakes the jug and the ice clunks, taunting them. He tosses the bottle aside.

The sky is dark now, and except for the flashlight, everything inside is black — black and cold; the red tips from their cigarettes glow eerily, illuminating lips, chins, and noses. The men become faces floating in the blackness, without bodies, without eyes. Outside the wind is howling and whistling around the aircraft. Like fingers, the wind finds every crack in the hull of the bomber and cold air slithers into the interior of the plane. The men shiver, slapping their arms, stamping their feet, and walking around to bring life back into numb body parts. They talk to keep themselves awake. They talk about their homes and families, their childhoods, and their first loves.

Dave climbs forward to check the airspeed indicator in the cockpit. It shows the wind at 120 kilometres per hour. He pulls the collar of his flight jacket closer around his neck.

Al gathers up the three parachutes and rips up two of them. The three men wrap themselves in the material until they all look like extras in a bad horror movie. The wind howls and the bomber shakes. Moving into the smaller wireless compartment, they keep close together so their combined body heat will help keep them from freezing. Every now and then one of them drifts off and gets slapped and yelled at. They regularly switch places, as the middle man stays the warmest. One of them reads the warning on the side of the chute pack and laughs, "This parachute is to be returned in 24 hours."

The wind whistles outside, and the men think they will go insane with the incessant howling.

Chain-smoking helps. Even Al, who has never smoked a day in his life, smokes with the others. Lighting one cigarette off the end of another, it helps to keep them awake. So does walking, kicking the sides of the plane, slapping each other on the back — any movement that keeps the blood flowing and their feet and hands from freezing.

Minus 38.

Taking what's left over from two of the chutes, they stuff bits of cloth in every crack and corner of the compartment to try and shut out the Arctic wind. They talk as they smoke, walking and keeping each other awake long after midnight.

Minus 41 degrees Celsius.

They are so thirsty, their conversation drifts to hot cups of coffee, tea, and hot cocoa. There is nothing to drink, until one of them notices that the condensation from their breath is sticking to the metal of the plane and forming a layer of ice. The survival guides all say not to melt ice in the mouth as it drops your body temperature. But the air is frozen dry, and they are so thirsty. Chipping off bits of the ice with awkward fingers, they suck on it. Their mouths get sore from the ice, but it's all they have. As the night continues, talking becomes difficult. The violence of their shivering makes them stutter and brings on sputters of laughter that only partially ward off the fear of dying.

At about 3 a.m. David drags out the food rations: 24 hard tack biscuits, also frozen. With no idea how long they could be there before help arrives, half a biscuit each every 24 hours will have to do. That gives the air force 16 days to find them before they run out of food. As long as they can stay awake and take in enough moisture, they can live a long time without eating. They act like the information is a relief, but no one wants to mention the weather. How long does it take for a man to finally succumb to the elements and freeze to death?

Gathering the biscuits together, the three crawl into the tail compartment, which is smaller still, and lay on top of each other to keep warm. Draping the last of the parachute material over themselves, they huddle close to keep their body heat in. At first it feels warm, but after they get used to it, they start shivering again. They shift positions, each taking a turn in the middle while the wind outsides continues to howl and shake the bomber.

Minus 42. The night seems endless.

Dave tells them about his last trip home to see his new baby girl; Al talks about his girlfriend in Michigan and worries about his newly widowed mother. He hopes she doesn't get the dreaded telegram before they're found.

Arthur tells the other two about his wedding a few months before. He talks about the drunk relatives and how beautiful his new bride was. He describes the mountains of food. There is an awkward pause, and Dave pulls out his daughter's picture. They all have a good look at it. They prop it up against the wall of the plane as a reminder — their loved ones are waiting for them to come back alive.

Dave looks at his watch; it reads 8 a.m. Even though it's still dark out, they pry open the door to see if they can see any lights or stars, or if there's been a change in the weather. The wind is still driving the snow across the ice, but the temperature has risen.

Minus 33 degrees Celsius.

It's one day that they have survived, one day closer to being rescued, and one day they'll never have to live through again. But they all know it's also probably the easiest day they'll have until they're rescued.

Day 2: –35 degrees Celsius.

It's dark by 5 p.m. As soon as the sun starts to set, the wind picks up again, and the temperature bottoms out. The wind pushes its way through the body of the plane and the drafts are unavoidable. The bomber trembles and shakes with it, making it feel like they're airborne. Closing their eyes for just a moment, they are in the sky above the clouds and flying home.

They are all but talked out. They doze for a few short minutes here and there, until one of the others shakes them awake. No one has had any real sleep. The hunger has turned to pain, and between shaking from the cold and moving to keep from freezing, all they can think or talk about is food.

For three days they wait, pacing like caged animals. Their thirst is constant and the ice chips from the walls are leaving ugly sores inside their mouths and around their lips. Fingers — frozen and warmed over and over — are split and red, stiff from the elements and aching from the cold.

On the third night, at about 11 p.m., the three men stop in their tracks and look at each other, stunned. Silence. The wind has stopped and the plane has stopped shaking. It takes all three of them to break the door open, sealed by the ice that was built up on the outside, before they can jump onto the crust swept clear by the wind. Al sets up his sextant and takes readings. He climbs back into the plane and madly scribbles down the information. According to his calculations, they are on Greenland inside the Arctic Circle, 24 kilometres from the Atlantic and 177 kilometres from the nearest civilization.

They look at each other. No one says it, but they all know that a 177-kilometre walk over the ice in this weather without food or water is suicide — they all look away. Staying here in this frozen metal coffin is suicide, too.

Finally, eyeing the rubber dinghy pack, they decide that 24 kilometres to the Atlantic is doable. With three of them paddling, 161 kilometres up the coast to civilization is a stretch, but possible. At least by walking they have a better chance than sitting on the ice waiting for someone to accidentally look in the right place.

Working through the night, they make five snowshoes out of some good-sized plywood box tops from the cargo on board. They fashion the sixth one out of the cushion in the cockpit. Then they tear the last parachute into thin strips for laces to tie the contraptions on their feet.

Loading up with the Very pistol and cartridges, three marine distress signals, the compass, and the pitiful supply of hard tack, they fill their pockets with cigarettes. They are ready to set out. Prying open the door to get an early start, they find the wind has picked up again during the night. The sky is again overcast and snow is flying in all directions. They could wander in circles in this weather and never be found. So, they close the door, unpack, and wait in silence, smoking, as the bomber starts to shiver again with the strength of the Arctic wind. They hate the wind. It's like an animal, a predator clawing at the door to get at them.

They are so cold, they can't feel their feet and fingers. Stamping around the fuselage is like walking on blocks of wood. Their breath puffs white mist; the metal walls and Plexiglas are coated with white ice about seven centimetres thick. Every minute drags on and the cold is so persistent, they can't escape it, not for a moment. No one speaks. They no longer have anything to talk about; they stop feeling hungry. Each hour they are delayed they became weaker, colder,

34

and closer to giving up. Soon they won't have the strength to walk 10 metres, and they need to go so much farther than that to find help. Does anyone even miss them or know where to look?

Unable to wait helplessly anymore, Arthur tinkers with the antennae that was damaged during the landing and plays with the radio, flicking the knobs and tapping the tubes. Suddenly, the air is filled with static, and the three gather hopefully around the set. Each holds his breath as Art fiddles with more wires and knobs. Suddenly, there it is. Almost drowned out by the static, they hear a distinct tapping of Morse code!

Arthur breaks in on the line with their SOS and position. The tapping carries on without a pause. He tries again, fingers so frozen he's hitting the keys with his fist, "SOS," "SOS," followed by their position. Arthur yells as he pounds out the message. He stops. There's a momentary silence, then, mixed with the static, comes a response: "RR" (meaning they've been heard and the other end has the information). Then the battery dies, and again the radio is dead. Only 90 seconds, but they were heard.

They look at each other. Now what? How long before help arrives? If the rescuers can't find them or the weather decides not to cooperate, how much longer can they hold on? A rescue plane couldn't possibly land in these conditions and get airborne again. If the weather takes another turn for the worse, no one will be able to hike in. No one will be able to see them from above either. They have to get out of the plane and get to a place where they can be found, where they can be reached and taken off this damn hunk of ice.

They talk, they stomp, they nibble on their ration of biscuits, now cut back to one quarter per 24 hours, and they smoke. The wind howls outside; the snow blows in thick gusts making the plane shiver and rattle. The temperature continues to drop.

Minus 38.9 degrees Celsius.

The bomber is like a freezer. They feel like trapped animals. The more they breathe, the thicker the ice coats the windows, and the harder it is for them to see outside. They can't risk sleeping; all they can do is pace and smoke and wait. Now and again one of them talks gibberish, as if he's somewhere else. The others coax him to his feet and with the movement, lucidity returns. Each time it happens, they wonder how long it will be before there's no coming back from that world.

No matter how much ice they suck, their thirst is unquenchable. They move in a state of numbness. They aren't tired any more, nor are they hungry. Slowly, they're dying, freezing to death, and none of them can do anything about it.

Day six. The weather clears up. They inflate the dinghy with the carbon-dioxide cartridge and burn all the official papers on board. Using the flames to defrost the coffee flasks, they manage to share a cup between them — all they could melt — but it is the best coffee they have ever had. Lukewarm, it still warms and gives them hope.

Loaded up and ready at last, they leave the plane at 1 p.m. The snow is deep, and while the snowshoes help, they're ponderous and the men are weak. The dinghy is supposed to ride on top of the snow, but in reality drags behind heavily. The men have to stop every 40 metres or so to rest. In two hours they've only covered half a kilometre and the 24-kilometre trek left to go starts looking impossible to manage. Arthur sees an aircraft about 10 kilometres away, and they fire off a flare. The plane keeps going and the three realize they haven't been seen. Then it begins to snow again. They look at each other and turn around to return to the plane. Without the snow, they might make it; with it, they won't.

Plus 16.

Rain! The warmth feels like heaven as they step from the plane. They set out again with lighter hearts but a tougher trek. The snow is mushy and clings to everything.

Darkness falls and the wind starts up. They have only made two kilometres, but they are running out of survival time and turning back is no longer an option. The temperature drops and everything wet freezes. Propping up the dinghy on the boat paddles, they crouch in frozen clothing and boots for the next 17 hours of darkness. None of them thinks he will make it through the night. They shiver so badly, they clench their jaws to prevent their teeth from shattering against each other. Their flight suits freeze painfully to their skin, their eyelashes are white with ice, and the only shelter is in huddling together under the lee side of the rubber dinghy. They pray.

With daylight comes the surprise that they are still alive and then the devastation of finding long stretches of crevasses between them and the ocean. The 24-kilometre trek has doubled with detours around impossibly deep cuts in the glacier. Their route may even have tripled, but they need to go on. Behind them, waiting in the cold metal tomb of their downed bomber, lies death. Ahead of them might also be death, but at least they will go fighting to survive. And they have to survive — their families are waiting for them.

Two kilometres around the first crevasse they stop to stare at the sky. They look at each other, making sure they all heard the sound — a plane!

The three lunge for the dinghy and the flares. The first cartridge misfires and frozen fingers fumble with the second one. They load, point to the sky, but nothing happens. Almost in tears, fingers even clumsier, they load the third and last flare, pistol cocked. Up it goes with a bang and a drawn-out fizz. The three hold their breath and wait. Did the pilot see the flare? Was it too late? Is the plane circling?

Yes!

Low above them, the plane banks around then comes back again, wagging his wings and dropping small parachutes with bundles dangling from them. The three race forward like drunks on their makeshift snowshoes to tear open the parcels like excited children. Food, clothing, sleeping bags, real snowshoes, rope, instructions, and a bottle of Scotch!

Al can't stop himself. He has never tasted liquor in his life, but it's liquid and he's so thirsty; he pulls off the cap and downs about a quarter of a litre before the other two stop him. Dazed, he stands for a moment, then sits down hard on the snow with a weird look on his face and falls over. He rolls onto his back, smiling through cracked lips, and falls fast asleep.

Worried that Al will freeze, Arthur tries to shake him awake. But after nine sleepless days and nights, nothing is going to bring him to. David and Arthur get him out of his wet clothes, into dry ones, and then into a parka. Rolling him, still sleeping soundly, they zip him into a cozy sleeping bag and leave him be.

Although sleep is tempting, David and Arthur are suddenly hungry. Changing into dry clothes, they open up the U.S. Army "K" rations and eat three full meals before stopping.

Warmer, dry, and with full stomachs, they turn to the note that accompanied the parcels. It instructs them to tie themselves together and walk in a straight line to the ocean where a Coast Guard vessel will be waiting for them.

Since Al is already asleep, Arthur and David decide to nap as well before setting out again, and they crawl into the other two sleeping bags.

About an hour later, Arthur wakes up with terrible

stomach pains. Crawling frantically out of the sleeping bag, he starts retching violently. A few minutes later, moaning and clutching his stomach, David joins him. All the noise wakes Al. He finds the food and eats ravenously. A few minutes later he too is vomiting, probably more from the Scotch than from the food.

Gathering what they need, they leave the dinghy and the homemade snowshoes behind in a pile. The new snowshoes work better, and they travel faster. With darkness comes rain. They wish they had kept the dinghy for shelter. Since everything is wet and freezing with the dropping temperature, they stand.

The next day the fog is so thick, they're afraid to move. The number of crevasses increases the closer they get to the coast, and they're afraid they will fall in one without seeing it. Finally, the fog clears in the afternoon and, leaving the wet sleeping bags behind, they start to the coast.

That night the temperature plummets and the three huddle together with arms around one another. An hour later they're frozen together and can't break free. Struggling and swearing, they finally break apart.

Arthur drifts off for a bit, until David, afraid he'll freeze to death, shakes him awake. Arthur stands up to move around and finds his foot feels dead, like standing on a block of ice. Pulling off his boot, his foot is white and lifeless. Even the angry sores from being frozen so many times are white. Dave and Al rub the foot, blow hot breath on it, and rub it some more. After an hour the feeling starts to come back and the pain sets in.

The next night, the three feel the earth move as the ice beneath them starts to heave. Standing close together, they hear a low, long groan. Every hour or so, a thunderous crack echoes across the glacier and the ground shifts and shivers. The men sing to ease their nerves and drown out some of the noise as they wait for daylight.

Morning shines bright and clear. Despite their exhaustion, the men feel like they can almost fly over the hard-crusted snow, stopping only for short breaks. Rescue is within their reach, and none of them wants to spend one more night in the open. They leave behind everything that is slowing them down.

Late in the afternoon they spot a boat about 22 kilometres off the ice field. The three run, stumbling forward as quickly as they can. Suddenly they stop — they are on top of a 90-metre ice cliff. Below them is the crashing sea. The boat, bobbing in the waves, is obviously waiting for them. But they have no way of signalling it. All they have is David's lighter.

Stripping off his parka, Arthur pulls apart the stuffing to set it on fire with the lighter. The parka smoulders, but is too damp to burn. They try the other two with no better luck. The men just stand there, not knowing how to let the boat know they're there.

About 7 p.m., the boat shoots off a number of flares high into the sky and sweeps a searchlight along the coast, missing the men with every sweep. Arthur, David, and Al jump up and down, waving their arms, and yelling with all their strength. But the searchlight continues to miss them. They are too high and too small to see, especially in the dark.

Above them, they hear a familiar throb of an airplane engine. The plane heads out to the boat, and the boat turns around to go back out to sea. The men watch helplessly as both disappear. Sitting down, they strip off the parkas and tear them into small pieces, piling the driest material together in a pile. This is their last chance for rescue.

Determined, they cuff their hands around the lighter, putting it to the material. First, a small spark, and the soft stuffing crackles; then there's a flare-up, *poof,* and a fizzle with a small puff of smoke as it goes out. The lighter is almost out of fuel, and the flame dies. David clicks it; there's a spark but no flame. Again and again and again, spark but no flame, then a small flicker wavers uncertainly in the darkness. Gently holding it to the pile of material, they hold their breath — *poof!* The cloth catches almost immediately. The men yell and slap each other on the back. Tearing up more of the parkas, they feed the fire until it's roaring. Facing the black ocean, they whistle and yell, feed more cloth into the fire, and turn and yell some more. Within minutes, a flare shoots high into the sky from the boat. A signal light flashes out Morse code: "Move back from edge of glacier and bear south to meet landing party."

Their progress is slow and cold. Having burned their

parkas, there's little to keep out the Arctic cold, and the ice cliff is slippery. In the dark, the crevasses are on all their minds, as is the possibility of sliding off the cliff into the ocean below.

Around 9:30 p.m., the sound of voices reaches their ears. They climb down to a low part of the cliff only a few metres above the water line, and a small boat comes into view. Before the men can adjust to the realization, they have been rescued, clumping their way with frozen feet onto the deck of the U.S. cutter. Their eyes shine over-bright from lack of sleep; their clothes hang loosely and flap limply as they move forward. It seems like a dream. None of them looks at the other in case they really are dreaming. But it isn't a dream; they are finally safe and warm after 14 days of frozen hell.

Chapter 3
From the Ice of the Arctic to the Heat of Battle

t took months for Arthur Weaver to feel warm again, as though the snow and howling wind had settled in his bones. His experience in Greenland leaves him sleepless at night, waking every hour or so disoriented, thinking he is back on the glacier. The damp weather in England, where he is stationed now, doesn't help. He still chills easily, finding it worst at times like this, when he's flying at 20,000 feet in –28 degrees Celsius.

Suddenly he hears the mid-upper yelling in the inter-com. A German night-fighter is coming at them from under-neath the plane. The rear-gunner swivels the turret to get a bead on the attacker. The gunner yells for the pilot to cork-screw, but the plane responds too late as anti-aircraft fire rakes the heavy from cockpit to tail. Another burst of machine gun fire crackles as Doug, the pilot, dives and corkscrews to starboard then twists once more. Arthur feels a red hot pain in his left side. The plane jumps and gyrates and he hangs on to the contents of his stomach as warm blood seeps through his flight suit and down his leg into his boot. He's been hit.

Tonight, January 30, 1944, they are on a bombing run to Berlin.

Arthur had an uneasy feeling before leaving on this ops. Riding the transport to dispersal, he could feel the cold seeping into his bones as the daylight faded to twilight. The WAAF (Women's Auxiliary Air Force) driving the transport smiled at him as he and the crew disembarked. He took the last puff off his cigarette and stomped it out under the heel of his boot. His stomach was flipping a bit more than usual as he looked to the eastern sky.

Flying Officer Douglas Edmund Biden is the pilot. They are flying out on Lancaster D (for Daisy) with No. 405 Squadron. Doug is from Moncton, New Brunswick. The guys call Doug "cat" behind his back; he's had so many near misses they figure he has nine lives. Arthur hopes that tonight he's got some of those lives left. Berlin is always a nasty target.

Tonight is his third mission flying in a Lancaster with the Pathfinders. His unit is in front of the bomber stream and has the job of dropping flares to guide the planes to the targets. Then they'll hang around for a bit and re-mark the area as the bombs extinguish the markers. The Pathfinders always

A Lancaster bomber

seem to be in the worst of the battle at the worst times. Night fighters buzz after them first. If the enemy can knock out the Pathfinders, then the bombers won't know where to drop their bombs.

Behind Daisy is a bomber stream 534 aircraft strong. There are 440 Lancasters and 82 Halifaxes, with 12 Mosquitoes as escorts.

Nearing the enemy coast, the aircraft has already run into trouble. Down below, some German is awake and lets loose his anti-aircraft guns to add to the stress, missing, but making the wounded bomber jump. The night-fighter took out one engine; Daisy, billowing smoke, is an easy target. The crew wonders if they will be heading home or carrying on to the drop zone. Then the night-fighter comes at them again, peppering the underbelly once more. Both gunners open fire, and the German heads for the horizon. Doug doesn't turn back, but carries on. They should have known that Doug would never turn back from a fight.

The damage report isn't good. Not only is the engine down, the bullets hit two fuel tanks, and gas is pouring out below. It doesn't take long to find out the electrical system is out as well. Suddenly, the bomber lurches as the bombing doors drop. The hydraulics have cut out, and the gun turrets are unable to swivel. The gunners will have to crank them around by hand.

Arthur was thrown to the floor with the last round. He pulls himself up, a bit dazed, and then feels more warm blood seeping through his clothing. His side burns, and stabbing pains shoot up into his chest. He's having difficulty breathing and every time he moves there's a fresh gush of blood that leaves him light-headed. He grabs a field dressing and stuffs it against the wound, wrapping it around his waist tightly. The support feels better and seems to stem the blood flow. Moving carefully and very gently, he takes his seat at the wireless once more. Injured or not, he has a job to do; for the crew to make it home, a team effort is required.

Over the target, the Pathfinders drop their flares. With her job done, Daisy leaves the rest of the group to limp back to the airbase before she runs out of fuel. To make the gas last, Doug flies low, below the strong upper currents that would push him backward. But it's no use; there simply isn't enough to get them home.

Doug tells the crew to get their gear together — they have to ditch. The men hook up their parachutes, grab carbon dioxide bottles to inflate the dinghies, and make sure their Mae Wests are in place. At least if they don't make it, England is in sight — they could almost swim there.

That's all Arthur needs, a dunking in the frigid Atlantic. He decides not to report his injury to the pilot. He's afraid if Doug knows, the injury will slow them down and hinder the rest from making it to shore. He doesn't want the pilot to risk the lives of the rest of the crew by deciding to try to make it to a base to save him. Arthur knows the chances are against him in the ocean. Shock will set in, and he's lost enough blood to interfere with his ability to swim. But the ocean is softer than the hard ground, and landing on an airstrip with the bombing doors open could eliminate any chance of survival for all of them.

Miraculously though, Daisy makes it to land. Arthur tells Doug the closest air base is Middleton St. George; Doug instructs him to let the base know they are coming in on fumes, only three engines, inoperative hydraulics, and open bomb doors (so no landing gear). A messy belly landing is in their immediate future.

Arthur relays the message, and then, like the rest of the crew, straps in and braces for the worst.

Doug lines Daisy up, flying in on three engines. He trims and reduces speed. An engine sputters, and Doug takes her down quickly, before another one dies. The plane hits the tarmac with the impact of a freight train. Sparks fly out from behind, and the undercarriage shakes, shudders, and groans with the friction of asphalt against steel. The kite turns as it careens down the length of the runway at 120 kilometres per hour. Emergency vehicles follow in her wake: fire, ambulance, and sand trucks. Daisy slows, and one wing tilts sideways. The underbelly is red hot, and smoke billows into the sky. The crew hold their breath. If the wing buckles before they stop, the remaining fumes in the fuel tank could blow them all to hell. An empty tank has more explosive power than a full one; right now that tank is nothing but flammable fumes, under pressure, and ready to blow. But Daisy seems to drift across the ground in slow motion, turns completely around, and settles with a groan. Firemen leap out of the truck and begin to hose down the plane. The crew pops out the front window, and crawls to safety.

Arthur needs help badly — blood loss and pain make it impossible for him to jump out on his own steam. He lets the pilot know he's injured, and he's gently lowered through the window into the arms of the medics. He spends time in hospital recovering from his wounds, but soon he's back on duty. Although he's still in pain and barely healed, he carries on without complaint.

Chapter 4
Czech Refugee Fights as a Proud Canadian

or Vladimir V. Havlicek (Dimi), born in Prague, October 23, 1909, and raised in Czechoslovakia, the announcement over the radio that the Nazis have invaded his homeland is a death sentence. The European unrest started while he was a student at the university in Prague. For the countries close to Germany, the threat of invasion was always very real, and Dimi knows that his small country will need a strong military to fend off the German appetite for land and power.

But with no outside support, the resistance to the Nazis' invasion is short-lived. Czech officers soon start to disappear, and Dimi knows his turn is coming. During his mandatory term in the military, Dimi earned his officer status. Rumour has it that any officers from the Czech Militia will be disposed of.

Dimi and his fiancée Marie decide their only chance for life is to escape the country. Britain is too close to the German threat and hadn't lifted a finger to stop the Germans from advancing on the Czechs. He and Marie decide that Canada is their best chance.

Gathering only what they can conceal in their pockets, they leave their apartment in the middle of the night. Trying to look as casual as possible, they hold hands and whisper like lovers out on the town. Travelling mostly at night, they make it to the Austrian border. Purchasing skis and a few items from a merchant, they finally feel close to safety. For a few days they lay low, watching German military movements to judge the best place to escape over the border. They pick a moonless night and wait for 1:30 a.m. to make their move.

Wearing dark clothing, they put on their skis and head for the border through a small forest. They almost make it when, breaking through the peaceful night comes a shout from behind them. The pair doesn't wait or hesitate — they make a mad dash for the border, thinking the skis will give them the advantage of speed. Another shout echoes through the trees, and then another. Dogs bark and a hail of bullets whiz past them, hitting trees with a ripping of wood and the snow with puffs of white. Dimi's adrenaline races as he feels a bullet tear through his lower leg, throwing him to the ground. Marie lets out a small cry and also falls. But Marie doesn't move after she hits the ground, and a dark pool quickly spreads in the snow around her still body. Dimi knows she is gone. Grief hits the pit of his stomach and he hesitates for a moment, but he can't help her now and if he doesn't keep going, he will die with her.

Dragging himself to his feet, he ignores the hot pain in his leg and races on his skis as fast as he can, reaching the safety of the border as bullets strafe the snowy track in his wake. He doesn't stop or look behind him.

Months later, finally in Canada, he feels he can stop running. Classed as a refugee, Dimi gets a job with the Bata Shoe Company in Toronto and falls in love with a model named Tone. Once again, war interrupts his life. The Hitler regime, ever hungry for more power, invades Poland on September 1, 1939. Following Britain's lead, on September 10, Canada declares war, and Dimi joins the Royal Canadian Air Force.

In March 1941, Dimi finds himself a navigator with Coastal Command in No. 240 Squadron flying in Supermarine Stranraer aircraft. These are double-winged planes with wire supports between the upper and lower wing on either side. These twin Bristol Pegasus engine biplanes are outfitted with pontoons for landing on the water and are nicknamed "flying boats."

There's no ocean storm like a winter one off the coast of Scotland. With the open Atlantic knocking at the door, the wind kicks up huge waves with valleys so deep that ships disappear from sight only to reappear high on the rise of a new swell. Navigation is almost impossible; crews are kept busy trying to stay afloat.

For some reason, 1941 is a particularly bad year for storms. Rain mixed with snow, wind chill below zero, and the Atlantic surf that hammers the coastline has ships and aircraft grounded. It's a horrible night for the call Coastal Command receives at No. 240 Squadron stationed at Stranraer, Scotland, that February.

A disabled ship is floundering about 500 kilometres off the coast, somewhere amid the ocean turmoil of waves, wind, and freezing rain. The navy doesn't have a ship close enough to reach the vessel in time, and officers anticipate having trouble finding the ship in the high seas. All inland aircraft are grounded due to the wind. Can Coastal Command help?

Flight Lieutenant Vince Furlong, a veteran peacetime-trained pilot, and Navigator Dimi Havlicek confer over maps and charts, calculating the wind and mileage with the last known coordinates of the floundering ship. They decide that if they can get their flying boat out of the water and airborne, they can make it to the stranded ship in time.

Within minutes, the six-man crew — Furlong and Havlicek, along with British radio operator Sergeant Harry Harley Newbury, and three gunners, Canadian Sergeant Matthew Gordon Wilson, British Sergeant Joseph Leslie Elwell, and British Sergeant John Sterling Hesk — are suited, fuelled, and ready to attempt a takeoff.

The weather is wicked; waves crash on the shoreline and the chop makes taxiing out a challenge in itself, even though the dock sits in a protected inlet.

The pilot revs the two engines positioned on the upper wing above and on either side of the cockpit. The plane races along the water, bouncing and crashing on each wave. The wind buffets the nose in unexpected gusts, making it hard to judge its direction. The first attempt to lift off fails. The pilot swings around for a second try, taxiing to the end of the bay and around to face the wind again. Once more the engines whine. Fighting the wind, the aircraft thunders over the waves, gaining enough momentum to skim the top of the swells. It looks good, until a gust of wind catches the wing tip, and the aircraft almost flips over.

Cursing and perspiring, the pilot turns the flying boat around once more. If they don't find the ship and it sinks, searching for survivors in this storm will be impossible. With renewed determination, the pilot faces the wind and waves. Racing for the sky, the craft is bashed brutally as the chop grabs at the pontoons. The engines whine as the plane thunders through the swells. It lifts, planes, and finally finds air. The wind catches the wings, and the flying boat bucks and jumps. The pilot fights the stick, using his feet to work the flaps, keeps the nose up, and counters the gusts to retain control. Everyone hangs on for dear life as the plane seems to go in all directions at once. Freezing rain splatters over the Plexiglas windshield, making visibility extremely poor. Using mainly a compass, they head out to sea and climb only high enough above the waves to keep the surface visible. Closing in on the coordinates of the last communication, all eyes are on the surf below, looking for anything resembling a ship. They hope they aren't too late.

Hours later they radio back to base. The ship is swamped but still afloat, and the Stranraer is in contact with the navy. They will keep circling the vessel to help the navy find it in the swells.

The navy finally arrives, and the plane banks for home. But while they were busy with the floundering ship, the wind changed direction and is now hitting them head on. The engines throb and strain to make headway as the wind and rain pound, trying to push them backward. The flying boat moves forward very slowly, but their fuel gauge drops quickly. As the hours pass, the storm grows in intensity, and the pilot realizes the inevitable. In these conditions, they will never make it home on the gas they have left.

Moving forward from his navigator's table, Dimi leans over the pilot and asks what the fuel gauge is reading.

Furlong checks the instrument panel and says there is only half an hour left, at the most. Home is only 33 kilometres away, but might as well be 300 with this wind blowing them in the face.

The two men share a look. The only alternative is to ditch while there is still enough fuel to control the landing. With the ocean this rough, though, luck is the only thing that will get them down in one piece. If the plane sinks, the men will be dumped into the freezing ocean, and rescue will most likely turn into a body recovery mission.

"Prepare for ditching," the pilot grimly announces.

Sergeant Pete Hewitt jettisons the depth charge load to prevent it from exploding when they hit the water. The aircraft jumps from the sudden loss of weight and Furlong re-trims while the twin Pegasus engines throb steadily on. The crew silently prepares for the worst. At any speed, hitting the water in this weather will like ramming the ground.

In the blackness of the storm, 100 metres below, the churning, foaming mass of giant waves reaches up for the human lives hovering slightly beyond its grasp. Thick, wet snowflakes replace the freezing rain and pitch crazily into the windshield from all angles.

"Okay, everybody," Furlong's very English voice comes over the intercom, "Mae Wests on; ready for ditching in a few minutes. You all know your stations and the drill. Elwell, Wilson, Hesk — don't forget the rations, water, and signals — and make sure the oars, life-lines, and bellows are in the dinghies. Dimi, remember the Very pistol and cartridges — and give your latest position to Newbury. Newbury, start sending your SOS and position in plain language. In this weather, rescue is rescue no matter which side finds us." The thought of the Germans picking them up doesn't please Dimi.

Pete Hewitt stuffs the Syko coding machine into a weighted canvas bag, along with the secret code cards and documents. Its destination is the ocean floor, where it can't fall into enemy hands.

Everything seems ready when, as the crew sits tensely waiting, a plaintive, desperate voice sounds over the intercom.

"Elwell here, sir. I — I forgot my Mae West and I can't swim!"

There is a long silence. All extra weight was stripped from the aircraft to compensate for the weight of the ammunition. Each crew member is responsible for his own survival kit.

After a few moments, Dimi's voice comes over the headphones. He's giving up his life jacket for Elwell.

"I can swim better than all of you put together," he says.

Ten kilometres from the Corswall lighthouse off the coast, the port engine sputters. The pilot orders everyone into crash positions and starts to take the flying boat down.

Heading dead into the wind, Furlong gives the okay and Hewitt drops three flame floats five seconds apart to mark the surface so the pilot can judge the landing better. Then he fires a couple of parachute flares into the air in case there is a ship or plane nearby. The flying boat does a tight 360 and Furlong inches it down toward the flares, fighting to keep it level so they have a chance at landing in one piece. The crew brace themselves and hang on tight.

Easing back on the throttles and slowly drawing the stick back toward his stomach, the pilot eyeballs the average height of the moving surface. He knows he will only have one shot, and a failed attempt will mean they all get wet. Survival in the Atlantic in this weather is an hour at the most. An injury could shorten that time considerably. The pilot not only has his own survival in his hands, he also has the lives of his crew.

The impact of water against steel thunders with freight-train intensity. The hull of the old Stranraer shudders and roars, straining and twisting as the first wave hits. The nose leaps forward into the air and crashes into the next wave, which splashes up and over, submerging the craft. It leaps up through the water and back into the air with the forward momentum, bucking and twisting in a way that steel was never meant to move. For an endless moment it hangs motionless above the water and then smashes against the surface in a final death throe. The crew battles to stay seated, belts straining to hold their bodies back from flying through the air. The pilot and co-pilot struggle with the controls, wrists yanking as waves grab and jerk the column out of their grasp. The third wave hits them broadside, and the ocean hangs on to the plane, weighting it to the water's surface. Miraculously, dented and torn, the aircraft is still afloat and in one piece. Water squirts in through the hull where seams have sprung open with the impact, and slowly the flying boat starts listing dangerously to starboard. One pontoon is missing, the starboard wing-tip float is smashed, and the water is claiming victory as it sucks the wing below the surface. In a few minutes the float will fill with water and the plane will capsize with the first wave that hits the broadside. For a short time the engines will keep them headed into the wind, but as the fuel runs out, it'll be at the mercy of the sea.

Elwell tosses the drogues (long canvas tubes) out from the nose. Usually they trail behind the aircraft to act as brakes. Throwing the drogues from the nose will keep the plane facing into the wind when the engines quit.

Leaping up from their crash positions, the crew inflates the rubber dinghies ready for launching. They all know that life expectancy in that heaving, frothing ice water will be measured in mere minutes, perhaps even seconds. Their only real hope lies in keeping the plane afloat until the storm blows itself out. Newbury and Hesk start up the auxiliary power unit and hook it up to the bilge pump. Every free hand is bailing water, but it flows in faster than it can be thrown out. As long as the plane is tilting into the water, the waves will win.

Dimi grabs a length of rope, coiling one end over his arm and the other around his waist. Climbing out through the escape hatch at the top of the plane, he inches out from the main body onto the upper wing. Hanging on for dear life, he crawls on his belly around to the other side of the engine. Carefully, he lowers himself onto the wildly pitching lower wing tilting upward at a 30-degree angle. Fastening the free end of his waist-rope around the nearest strut, he begins to thread his way through the struts toward the outer wing-tip. As he moves away from the body of the aircraft, the plane starts to shift with his weight, until the submerged opposite wing is lifting slightly clear of the surface of the water.

Wind and waves tear angrily at him, trying to dislodge him, but Dimi is determined. Reaching the end, he lies down and lashes himself to the wing and the struts. Even though water is still seeping into the plane, it has slowed enough for the pump and the bailing to keep up with it.

Realizing something has slowed the flooding, the crew look around with puzzled expressions. The pilot points to Dimi, tied firmly to the wing as the waves crash over him and the wind drives freezing snow in his face. Dimi lifts his hand and waves. They look in stunned disbelief knowing that if any of them survive this ordeal, it will be because of him. If they aren't rescued soon, they also know that Dimi's survival is doubtful.

Both engines sputter and die.

The pilot sits at his station and works the pedals continually to keep the rudders straight and the plane heading into the waves. Every now and again, he lifts his hand and waves to Dimi, and Dimi waves back. About an hour after he crawled out, Dimi stops waving. Tied to the wing struts, he rolls back and forth with each wave that crashes over it. No one can help him, even though they all have a chance to survive because of him.

All night the waves wash seawater into the plane; all night the crew bails it out. At one point, they talk about one of them taking Dimi's place, but realize it would take two people to bring his unconscious body in, and with that much extra weight on one side, the plane would tilt and capsize. Besides, after all this time, Dimi is probably already dead.

As dawn penetrates the darkness, the crew suddenly pitches onto the floor to the accompaniment of a horrendous grinding from below. The aircraft heaves high in the air and then comes crashing down with a sickening roar, twisting and tilting sharply to starboard. Everyone thinks it is coming apart and expects to see waves crashing in on them at any moment. Preparing for the worst, they brace for the impact. Nothing happens, however, except for a low groan as the old Stranraer settles, then rocks gently from side to side.

Somehow, against all odds, they drifted more than 90 kilometres and washed ashore on a tiny sand spit jutting out from Mull of Kintyre, one of the last points of land in the North Channel before it pours into the open Atlantic. It's a mere 90 metres wide. If they had missed this spot, they would have been either smashed to pieces on the rocks or washed out to sea.

Scrambling out to the end of the wing, the crew cuts down Dimi's limp body. Fearing the worst, they carry him onto dry land and check for a pulse. He's alive!

Stripping off his wet clothes, they wrap him in a dry blanket. Furlong and Newbury set off to the nearest town, leaving the others with Dimi. After they are rescued, Furlong requests that Dimi be decorated for his heroism. Sadly, he is overlooked.

Newbury dies shortly after in a ditching on March 21, 1941, and Elwell, Wilson, and Hesk also die, but in a different crash on May 7, 1941.

Dimi dies a hero's death a few months later on December 23, 1941. His plane ditched and while a couple of crew members managed to escape the plane, Dimi went back for a wireless operator unconscious at his station. Unstrapping him, Dimi dragged him forward and shoved him up through the hatch where the others hauled him to safety. Dimi disappeared back into the plane to make sure everyone else was out. He perished with four others.

Dimi's best friend, Navigator John A. Iverach RCAF, declared that Vladimir Havlicek could not have been more patriotic than if he had been born Canadian. Flying Officer Vladimir Havlicek, service number J3112, is buried in Runnymede Memorial Cemetery, listed as a Canadian.

Chapter 5
Unrecognized Patriotic Sacrifice

neisenau — the name of the great battle cruiser — strikes fear in the bravest of the British forces. Heavily guarded, the magnificent killing machine, along with her sister ship, the Scharnhorst, sits in dry dock at Brest waiting impatiently for the day they are once again unleashed in the battles waging around them. These ships are the greatest threat to Britain and her allies. They have already wreacked havoc on the British fleet; No. 22 Squadron of Coastal Command is on constant standby to strike at any German naval activity, either at sea or in well-defended coastal ports. So, no one is surprised when the battle order is posted, stating "at all costs."

Pilot Ken Campbell (Scottish) and his crew, Navigator Jim Scott (Canadian), Wireless Operator William Cecil Mulliss

(British), and Air-gunner Ralph Walter Hillman (British) are up early. The four head out from dispersal in the pre-dawn mist at North Coates air base. They are to be in the second wave of the attack. The first three aircraft carrying mines are to breach the torpedo nets and silence the flak ships to make way for the second attack of three torpedo bombers. Their orders are to bomb the battle cruisers while they lay dormant and trapped in port. Each aircraft is to take off independently and rendezvous near Brest. They are to fly in formation and then break to attack the ships in the harbour at first light. Their prime target is the Gneisenau.

The group is quiet. Only three light bombers are on this mission to attack the most intensely fortified harbour in Europe where the mightiest ships of the Third Reich's navy sit in port.

The airmen have the greatest confidence in their plane. The Bristol Beaufort — often referred to as a Torpedo Bomber — is a twin-engine plane with greater manoeuvrability than the Halifax and other heavy bombers. Although not as quick as a Hurricane or Spitfire, it fills the gap between fighters and bombers.

This isn't the first attack on the harbour since Gneisenau went into dry dock. Because of the intense Allied attacks on Brest, the port is on constant alert. A British bombing raid the previous day left an unexploded bomb on the dock next to the Gneisenau. The Germans defused the bomb and the most recent reconnaissance photos show that the Gneisenau

A Bristol Beaufighter

has been removed from the dry dock and moored out in the harbour in the shelter of a breakwater. This is the chance the Allies have been waiting for: the ship is more vulnerable now, and more accessible to attack.

None of the crew mentions what's on their minds, but all involved in the mission are aware that coming back is unlikely. At best, they may be shot down and live out the war as POWs. At worst, they won't survive at all. All four men know they are Britain's last chance to get rid of this threat. Damaging the ship to prevent her from continuing the destruction she has already caused to the British fleet is imperative. She has to be stopped from leaving the harbour and joining the others. The aircrew's prime objective is to get a clear run in with a torpedo and get out any way they can.

Suited up, parachutes tucked under their arms, the men climb aboard their aircraft. Ken takes his place in the cockpit after hanging his parachute behind his chair. Jim sits down next to the pilot in front of his navigation table. Although his role is navigation, he is also the bomb-aimer, and if necessary, the co-pilot. They strap themselves in.

Behind the pilot, William (Bill) Mulliss heats up his wireless set and slides his earphones over his head before strapping in. In the rear turret, Ralph Hillman checks his guns, locks down, puts on his headphones, and buckles up as well.

Due to bad weather, Campbell and his crew arrive alone at the grouping point off the harbour. After waiting for the others, they soon realize they aren't coming. They either go in alone or scrub the mission and turn back. They decide to go in and launch a single aircraft attack, knowing full well the harbour of Brest is the most heavily armoured area of the Third Reich. Bracing themselves for the inevitable blast from the shore and ship guns defending the area, they burst through the cloud cover as dawn breaks. Hoping surprise is still with them, they circle quickly to get into position for their run.

The harbour is protected on either side by curved strips of land dotted with clusters of gun batteries facing both the sea and inland. Along the north side of the harbour is a stone breakwater coming out into the bay and bending back toward shore. It's in this protected area of water where the small torpedo bomber spots the great ship secured along a wall on the north side. Behind her, rising sinisterly along the shoreline, stand more guns. Near the ship are three heavily armed anti-aircraft ships (flak ships), guarding the battle cruiser.

None of what they see is a surprise to the crew. They are there to do a job, and that's what they plan on doing. The only way to make it past the defences is to fly in low and fast, deliver the torpedo and pull up quickly in order to miss crashing into the wall, then bank sharply toward land and take their chances against the shore batteries.

The bomber sweeps in, skimming low over the water. James takes the aim while Ken flies the plane in front of the anti-aircraft ships, directly in front of their ominous guns. The brazen attack is a surprise for the Germans, who race to their positions on the flak ships as the bomber flies over the barrels of their guns. As Ken barely clears the breakwater, James lines up the shot and tells the pilot to let fly the torpedo from 460 metres. The plane jumps as the torpedo takes air. Water splashes when the missile breaks the surface and then whooshes up as she hits the ship's stern below the water level. The explosion blows a hole in the hull and damages the propeller. The great ship starts taking on water immediately as the guns from the three flak ships let blaze into the small torpedo bomber, raking it front to back. Ken banks the plane toward land as it is peppered with bullets. The bullets find their mark, killing Ken and wounding Mulliss and Hillman. Jim Scott pulls the body of his skipper and friend out of the cockpit and jumps into the pilot's chair. Strafed by thousands of enemy bullets, Jim pulls up to gain height as a German gunner lets fly his charge. There's a mighty *woof!* The small plane recoils as the shell smashes into the aircraft, ripping a large hole in the belly. Losing one engine, Jim makes a snap decision and aims the bomber straight down onto the deck of the German vessel. Some eyewitnesses in the French resistance onshore watch as the bomber explodes on impact, travelling across the deck and landing in the ocean, sinking with all crew members on board.

Photos taken later show the bomber's crash does very little damage to the cruiser's deck, but the hole in the hull from the torpedo disables the ship, and she starts sinking stern first. If she had been at sea, she would have gone down, but two of the harbour boats tow her back to shore where they pump out the water. Returning to dry-dock, she remains there for the next eight months, no doubt saving many Allied ships and men.

A year later, based on evidence collected from German prisoners of war and other witnesses, Campbell is post-humously awarded the Victoria Cross. There's no doubt in anyone's mind that he had heroically flown to the target and was killed by the anti-aircraft flak after the torpedo was off. But when the Germans recover the Beaufort out of the bay, they find to their surprise that Jim Scott is in the pilot's seat.

It is now known that it was the navigator, Jim Scott, who took over the bomber, guiding it to the deck of the Gneisenau in a further attempt to disable the vessel.

The pilot's VC is the first awarded to Coastal Command in the war. None of the other crew members were awarded a medal, but they all bravely gave up their lives for their country.

Chapter 6
Canada's First Score

ugust 15, 1940, is bright and sunny. It's the kind of day that pilots in the RCAF revel in. The few clouds languishing on the horizon are white and fluffy, and the ever-present breeze off the Atlantic drifts through the trees, encouraging the lazy, whimsical feel of England in the summer. Flying Officer Ernest McNab from Saskatchewan is thrilled to be leading his Canadian squadron into such a perfect sky.

The English countryside is charming when you tour it on the ground, but from the air, the fields and gardens below are woven together in quaint squares of colour with trees, so large on the ground, providing the border to the quilt. McNab loves to fly above the island simply to look at the beauty of it.

Then he sees something in the distance and feels his

heart skip a beat. With the intent of descending on London, a black cloud accompanied by the whir of German engines moves across the sky. Britain is being invaded by the Luftwaffe, and while McNab is only too aware of the "green" squadron following his lead, his job is clear — stop the enemy at any cost. Still he hesitates, but only for a second. This is only their second time up as a squadron, and engaging the enemy so quickly is daunting.

British planes are quickly finding air from bases all over England as the news of this daylight invasion shakes the military commanders. As the German twin-engine Dorniers inch closer to the city, the two sides collide in a twirling dance of death, both fighting desperately for air supremacy. The Germans are well-armed with more fire-power than the RAF, but not with more determination. This is the British homeland and the audacity of the brazen enemy forces has stimulated the English sense of pride. England will not belong to Germany as long as there is an Englishman alive and able to fight.

Over the Thames estuary, McNab singles out one of the German raiders. Adding throttle, he pulls up on the sun side of his target. Coming from the side, out of the sun, his Hurricane buzzes up the German's tail, shadowing every movement as they weave back and forth at crushing speeds. All McNab needs is enough time to get a bead on the enemy and then squeeze the trigger that feels so inviting under his fingers.

The Nazi pilot frantically corkscrews his fighter and rolls to throw off the Canadian bulldog. McNab hangs on and matches the German move for move, wheeling through the air in dizzying foreplay. By this time the din above the English countryside is deafening. The buzz of Hurricanes and Spitfires is punctuated with the throbbing Dorniers as fierce dogfights dominate the English airspace. Bombs drop on the British soil below, throwing debris and smoke skyward. Civilians flee in terror as bombs bounce and roll across the hills before detonating, leaving craters in their wake. German fighters strafe the roads below, sending motorists scurrying for cover. The dogfights in the air are punctuated with machine gun fire and death whistles as aircraft plummet to the ground.

McNab ignores the bedlam around him and concentrates on his personal encounter. He tries not to be overwhelmed by the ominous sight of those ugly black bombers fighting their way toward London, or to worry about his buddies, his friends, his men in the thick of the battle around him. This is their first taste of air combat, and they are in God's hands now. He knows that a war isn't won in one encounter, but one battle at a time.

His mouth dries up like cotton wool, and although he's only been engaged for minutes, it seems like hours of rolling, twisting, and turning as they fight to the death. Parachutes blossom all around, and explosions rock the ground as airplanes from both sides fall out of the air in broken pieces. He chases the Hun up into the sky. Above the clouds, they fight on in a world of their own. It's a world of freezing cold, of limitless space streaked with white trails of vapour and smoke behind reeling aircraft. It is also a world of solitude above the peaceful patchwork of English fields and a way of life that has been there for hundreds of years.

Finally, the invader in McNab's sights straightens for a moment — not a very long moment — but long enough for the Canadian ace from Saskatchewan to hit home with a short burst from his guns. The Nazi dives, pulls up, twists and turns for another bout of chase-me. Accepting the challenge, McNab weaves back and forth in his Hurricane behind the German and presses the trigger for a second scrappy burst. It's a hit, and the fighter spirals out of control, flipping end over end along the surface of the marshland, landing with a resounding crash followed by flames and smoke. Squadron Leader Ernest McNab has made the first score for Canada in what will be known as the Battle of Britain. He wags his wings in a moment of triumph, but only for a moment.

He has only just begun to hunt.

The taste of one fighter isn't enough when there are still so many of them vying for control of Britain. He spins off, and his squadron follows, covering his backside. He spots another fighter chasing one of their own. He pulls up and over, coming in from above and behind. He lets fly before the Dornier pilot even knows he's there. He fires; there's smoke and the German leaps from the plane to find the safety of the ground.

McNab and his men spread out as their fellow pilots pepper the air in parachutes. German planes are buzzing around the helpless men and gunning them as they hang suspended. Angered by the senseless butchery, McNab's men circle their comrades, keeping the invaders at bay until the men are safely on the ground. Then, they turn on the enemy with renewed vigour.

The fight only lasts a couple of hours, but they seem to pass as slowly as weeks. At long last, the locusts gather in a bedraggled cloud of defeat and limp back over the Channel whence they came. But not for long. The daring invasion continues through the rest of August, escalating with each episode.

August 30 is particularly intense. Raid after raid interrupts daily English life as successive waves of German planes fill the skies. The first air raid siren goes off early in the morning, followed by another, and then a few hours later another still. The fourth of the day's air raid warnings sounds loudly in London in the early afternoon as a huge force of planes is sighted over the English Channel. The First Fighter Squadron of the Royal Canadian Air Force, lead by Squadron Leader Ernest McNab, again leaps into the air to defend British air space. The bitter battle rages across the skies as the civilians below watch in horror and fascination. They are only too aware that their safety and future rests in the triggers of a few brave men in single-engine planes. The Nazis, determined to blow up a factory located only a few minutes away from the fighting, keep breaking away to make their bombing run. They are stopped short by the pesky fighters spitting and spinning in their wakes. Bomber formations break up time and time again, abandoning their bomb drops in order to shake off the fighters attacking the stream. The hot dogfights in the sky spike left and right until a line of smoke trails out behind, and a plane plummets to its explosive end.

Waves of Nazi aircraft roar over southeast England in a series of thrusts at the metropolitan area. Fighters engage the hostiles over London, over the Thames estuary, and meet them head-on over the Channel. Those on the ground take cover amid the roar of enemy planes and the staccato hammering of machine guns, never quite sure of their safety until the thud of bombs dropping far away tells them the battle has shifted position. At the end of the day the score is 42 lost for Germany, 12 for Britain, and the Jerries run home with their tails between their legs. Not for long. The Germans are determined to claim the British Isles for the Third Reich. The English, however, are even more determined to stop them.

On September 15, 1940, Germany launches an all-out daylight aerial attack. Throwing everything they have at the Brits to soften that stiff upper lip once and for all, the sky thunders as they pass. Civilians pour into the shelters to escape the onslaught, carrying what little they can with them. In shock at the intensity of the Nazi assault, they carry pictures, mementoes, a precious chair or heirloom. None of them knows what will be left of their homes or of England when they emerge. Will they have homes? A country?

The sirens herald the waves of incoming German

A Spitfire LF IX

aircraft, who in turn drop thousands of pounds of TNT, shattering brick buildings and leaving craters where neighbourhoods used to be. Powder drifts on the breeze, all that remains of 300-year-old buildings. In minutes, some areas of London are reduced to ruins. Thousands of people are dead or missing.

British, Canadian, and other Allied pilots scramble to their Hurricanes and Spitfires and meet the invaders head-on in bloody, spitting, screaming dogfights. Defending the innocent civilians below, the feisty fighters hit and run, grossly outnumbered, horribly out-gunned, but making up for it in aggressiveness and sheer cheek. Never staying still for long,

Canada's First Score

the Allies hit hard, then buzz away to the next, doing as much damage to as many planes in as short a time as they can.

Those fighting are awestruck by the magnitude of the attack and the heat of the defensive. There are more than a thousand aircraft filling the sky south of London. Planes are so close together and moving so quickly in attack and evasive manoeuvres that collisions and near misses happen in every direction. Those on the ground brave or curious enough to watch are stunned to see planes colliding in the air.

British Prime Minister Winston Churchill is in the command bunker deep below the streets of the city directing the defence. He's asked what resources Britain has to combat an attack such as this and replies, "There are none. The odds are great; our margins small; the stakes infinite."

Suddenly those around him have renewed respect for the fighting men in the skies. They are all that stand in the way of Germany and its plan to own the world.

Plane by plane, the fighters push the invasion back toward the Channel. The German planes, beaten and bruised, retreat, only to regroup and return two hours later. The Canadians and their Allied counterparts have just enough time to catch their second wind. They meet the next thrust of German offensive with a fierceness that sends the Germans home in 15 minutes. As quickly as they come, they leave, and suddenly aerial pandemonium is replaced by an empty blue sky with white, fluffy clouds resting on the horizon.

By the end of the day, Germany has lost over 60 aircraft

and failed to break through Britain's defences. Although nightly bombings continue to terrorize Britain, the daylight raids diminish until they stop altogether by mid-October. The Allies win this portion of the air battle of Britain, and 22 Canadian pilots lose their lives in doing so. Ernest McNab, firing the first shot for Canadians back home, continues his fight for freedom until he is sent home at the end of the war.

Chapter 7
Joining the Ranks of Canadian Aces

he gun turret of a bomber command aircraft during World War II is the coldest, most isolated place in the sky and one of the most dangerous. Over 20,000 air gunners lost their lives in their lonely turrets during the war. The mid-upper position was a little safer, but it didn't see quite the same amount of action since most enemy fighters attacked from the rear or from below, taking out the rear guns first. Once the rear gun is out, the underbelly and tail have limited protection, and the bomber becomes easy picking.

Most of the young men in gun turrets didn't know the odds. They simply focused on putting one foot in front of the other, hoping to make it home at the end of the war.

Peter Engbrecht, now manning the mid-upper gun

position of his Halifax aircrew, was born in Poltavka, Russia, in 1923. He and his family immigrated to Canada in 1926, settling in Whitewater, Manitoba. When World War II broke out, Peter was one of more than 3,000 Mennonites to turn their backs on their pacifist principles and join the fight for their country's freedom.

Gordon Gillanders, born in 1924, arrived overseas from Vancouver, British Columbia. He and Peter received their overseas posting in May 1944: No. 424 Squadron flying out of Skipton-on-Swale in the UK. By May 27, 1944, they receive their orders to attack Bourg-Leopold, Belgium. This is their second mission, and their crew is still considered green. Boarding their Halifax bomber nicknamed "Dipsy Doodle," neither of the two gunners has any idea what lies in store.

It starts out like any other night mission. The roar and thunder of 331 aircraft taking off shakes the ground, adding to the anxiety, excitement, and sometimes dread of the men going off to battle. Little do the men know that their mission tonight is only one of seventeen, and the enemy will fight long and hard on many fronts.

The Pathfinders arrive first at the target and drop flares for the bombers to find. They do their jobs well, accurately marking the target. With the night so clear, the bomber stream has little difficulty hitting the target.

Halifax HX316, Dipsy Doodle, drops the load as planned and Sergeant James Keyes, the pilot, heads the Halifax for home. The crew consists of Flight Sergeant Engbrecht (mid-upper gunner), Sergeant James G. Key (pilot), Pilot Officer Charles C. Gunn (wireless operator), Flying Officer Pat Peterson (bomb-aimer), Sergeant Charles Macdonald (flight engineer), Flying Officer William Riome (navigator), and bringing up the rear, Flight Sergeant Gordon Gillanders (rear-gunner).

Minutes after they head back to England, bullets whistle over them, and Engbrecht, manning the mid-upper guns, opens fire, aiming where the fiery tracer appears to originate from. He hasn't seen the fighter and reacts on gut instinct.

The enemy fighter banks around and comes in for the kill, making a bow attack. Gordon, in the rear-turret, yells into the intercom for James to corkscrew. Peter keeps up steady fire at the tracer, his bullets finding their mark. The Nazi plane drops off on one wing, obviously hit. The fuel explodes, and she goes down in a ball of flames, hitting the ground with another explosion. Neither gunner had seen the night-fighter, but the bomb-aimer got a glimpse of the fuselage and identified the enemy as a Messerschmitt 110 (Me110).

The night is alive with fighters. Dogfights between the enemy and the bomber's escorts chase erratically over the night sky. Smoke fills the air, from flak, anti-aircraft fire, and bombs exploding on the targets below. Like Dominion Day fireworks, the popping and gun bursts light up the night, followed by whistles and explosions below. It's hard to keep track of the identities of the planes in the air. Gunners keep their fingers on the trigger and their eyes peeled. Training never prepared them for the noise, the acrid smell of spent TNT, the bumping of flak, and the confusion in the darkness. The freezing cold that followed them from England is replaced now by nervous perspiration, hot flashes of adrenalin, and stiff muscles, aching from sitting tensely at attention as they comb the night for danger.

Straight out of the moonlight, a Junkers 88 buzzes for Dipsy Doodle. The fighter lines up the bomber in his sights and lets fly with both guns blazing. James yanks the bomber in a twist that sends everything and everyone tumbling. Peter and Gordon both open up with guns, and Gordon almost misses spotting the two other fighters — Me109s — coming in from below. The Junkers is only a decoy, and the ploy almost works. Gordon doesn't know why he looked beyond the obvious, but seeing the real danger from the other two attackers, he yells the warning. Peter swivels his four guns around and fires away. Gordon squeezes off round after round, and the three Germans swing away to re-group.

James decides to climb in case they come back.

Right on cue, the marauders come in again. Peter's guns jam, and with only one working, he continues to fire. Gordon swivels the rear turret to lend a hand. He lines up the enemy in his sights and squeezes his triggers, but nothing happens. All his guns are jammed and he can't clear them. All he can do is watch helplessly and yell evasive manoeuvres to the pilot. The plane grunts and groans heavily, as James twists and turns the lumbering metal giant. Rivets pop with the stress, sending screws pinging off into space. Stomachs flip. Flak explodes in the air around them, bumping and jarring the crew as they fight for their lives.

Peter's aim is good. He drives off the trio yet again, one gun to their four. But the night is not over, and the tenacity of the Nazis is obvious, as again, they close in from three different directions with guns blazing. Bullets rip down the side of the bomber in a staccato tattoo. James again jumps into action. The bomber has now lost all the altitude the pilot tried to gain. Flying below the height of the rest of the bomber stream, they are now sitting ducks. The night-fighters, tagging them as easy prey, are relentless. Sweating and swearing, James flies as he has never flown before. The crew is keenly aware that one bullet from the enemy could turn their aircraft, their friend and their protector, into their coffin.

Peter, with only one gun, fires whenever and wherever he sights an enemy plane. Again and again, Dipsy Doodle is attacked. Finally, over the English Channel, one of Gordon's guns becomes operational again, albeit sporadically. He's able to re-join the battle and help out the mid-upper, who feels like they're the prey in the annual turkey shoot at home.

Finally, the three fighters veer off and the crew starts to breathe a little easier. Their reprieve is short lived, however, as a Focke-Wulf 190 (FW190) flies in from above and attacks them on their port side. Peter fires straight into the tracer and the Focke-Wulf blows in a ball of shrapnel and flames. The original three attackers have now been replaced, and in packs of three, planes attack like wolves after a deer. James is unable to climb to escape the targeting, and frantically continues to twist and turn with every instruction his gunners give him. Peter is so busy shooting that he has no time to clear the jams from the other three guns and hopes with every round fired that his one last gun won't jam. Gordon yells instructions as another fighter closes in, but now the intercom is down and the pilot doesn't hear him. Passing the information by word of mouth, the two gunners and the pilot fight for their crew through a total of 14 attacks.

In the early morning hours, with England looming in the distance, the Germans relinquish their prey to fight another day. Dipsy Doodle and her crew limp home with battered and frayed nerves, but alive and all in one piece.

On August 7, 1944, flying in Halifax Galloping Gerty, Sergeant Engbrecht, supported by Sergeant Gordon Gillanders, shoots down another Me410 as well as a Ju88. At the age of 21, Peter Engbrecht, a member of a pacifist religious sect and of pure Germanic heritage, with five and a half enemy planes to his credit as well as two probables, becomes a Canadian RCAF Ace, the only one who isn't a fighter pilot. Throughout the war, Peter Engbrecht's accomplishments are unparalleled in the air force and he is awarded one of eight Conspicuous Gallantry Medals given to Canadians during World War II.

His team member and fellow Canadian Sergeant Gordon Gillanders finishes the war credited with three and a half enemy aircraft and is awarded the Distinguished Flying Medal.

Chapter 8
Escape

here's a full moon, and the men know the night's mission is a dangerous one. If they can see the target clearly, then they too can be clearly seen from below. The glint of grey metal against the backdrop of the silvery orb makes them sitting ducks for the enemy guns.

Squadron Leader Fletcher V. Taylor, a Canadian from Moose Jaw, Saskatchewan, paces uneasily at dispersal. It's cold, but it's not the air temperature he's feeling. His cold comes from the pit of his stomach. He prays his crew stays safe tonight.

Fletcher is with No. 420 Squadron out of Middleton St. George, England, flying a twin-engine Wellington with a bomber stream of 462 aircraft. He's got a good crew:

Pilot Officer and Navigator Crowthers; wireless air-gunner Sergeant McKinnon; mid-upper and ear-gunners, Pilot Officers Brown and Simpson.

Finally they receive the order to "stand by stations," and they board the aircraft quietly, strap in, and do their checks. When ready, Crowthers gives the ground crew the high sign, and the two men slowly crank the propellers to distribute the oil to the pistons and sleeves before start-up. The pilot switches on the ignition and presses the starter and booster-coil push buttons simultaneously for each engine in turn. Throbbing engines vibrate the air and make the ground tremble with the noise. The target for tonight is Stuttgart. It has been well marked by the Pathfinders.

The flight over is uneventful, and Fletcher laughingly tells himself to relax. Obviously, his apprehensions were unfounded; the enemy seems quiet and unaware of their approach. Although with that many aircraft in the air it's hard to imagine anyone being unaware of them.

Piece of cake. One by one the bombers dip over the target, level off, and drop their loads. A few night-fighters greet them but are quickly driven off by the Allied escorts. Fletcher banks and comes around, lines up on the target, and bombs away. Breathing a sigh of relief, he heads his crew for home.

Without warning, a ripping noise hits underneath the bomber as a Junkers 88 opens fire on them from behind and below. Bullets rip through the tail of the aircraft, setting the port engine and the wing on fire. Fletcher yells for reports on the damage and the enemy's location. The intercom is silent; he can only surmise the gunners have been hit. Hoping he's doing the right thing, he dives and corkscrews to shake off the predator he can't see. The pilot doesn't even know how long the wounded engine will continue to function and hopes the bomber will stand up to the gyrations he's putting it through.

There's a small explosion and shrapnel flies through the air. It's obvious the bomber is done for. Fletcher flips the switch on the bailout light, keeping the bomber as level as possible until Crowthers and McKinnon jump. Before jumping himself, Fletcher tries fighting the flames and smoke now overtaking the fuselage in order to rescue the gunners still in their turrets. The fire is out of control and the smoke is blinding; he can hardly breathe. Finally, he has to abandon the men and jump.

Suspended helplessly from his parachute, Fletcher watches his plane go down with the gunners still on board. If they were alive when he bailed, they would never survive the crash.

Fletcher lands in a field near Mesnil St. Denis, rolling as he hits the ground. Gathering up his chute, he runs to a nearby stand of trees and buries it in a pile of leaves. Somewhere in the night a dog barks and he feels a rush of adrenaline. Glancing at his compass and map, he jogs in the direction of the border. He knows there are resistance fighters in the vicinity; he just hopes he can find them.

When daylight starts to break, Fletcher crawls into a hollow under a large tree by a river bank. He tries to doze as he waits for darkness before travelling again. There are farms around, and now and again he can hear children playing close by.

For the next six days, Fletcher hides during the daylight hours and walks at night. His survival rations only last the first two days, and he gleans berries and raids gardens wherever he can. Finally he makes it as far as Soisson.

Exhausted, Fletcher stumbles onto the farm of Maurice Dupuis and takes a chance by contacting him. He's relieved to find the family are active members of the resistance; they will help him find his way back to England.

The farmer and his wife feed him well. After three days of laying low on the farm, Maurice and another man drive him to Laon, where Maurice gives Fletcher his own passport and a train ticket to Dole. Following Maurice's instructions, Fletcher leaves the train at Dole, and walks to Dijon to connect with more resistance fighters. From Dijon, he crosses over the Swiss border near Sainte-croix. On April 28, 1943, after eight months in Switzerland, he walks into occupied France with seven other airmen, the largest group to escape at once. The members of the group include Escape Party Commander Squadron Leader Fletcher Vaughan Taylor (Canadian), Flight Lieutenant George Frank Lambert (British), Second Lieutenant John Marshall Carah (American), Second Lieutenant Ralph Bruce (American), Flight Sergeant Hugh

Escape

Colhoun (Irish), Chief Petty Officer Donald Lister (Navy — British), Sergeant Stanley Herbert Kitchener Eyre (British), and Sergeant Richard Brown (British).

Under the cover of darkness, the group is loaded into a furniture truck and driven to the village of Frangy, Haute-Savoie, one of the strongholds of the French Marquis. This branch of the French resistance has more men and arms than any other branch.

The group of escapees then splits up. The half with Fletcher goes to the farm of C. Clement, while the other half are driven to an old warehouse in a quiet area on the outskirts of the village. Believing they are safe, the group beds down for a good night's sleep, leaving the leader of the resistance and Laurence Blanc on the outskirts of the village to guard them.

Early the next morning, the escapees in the warehouse are yanked from sleep as a group of men break in waving guns, yelling and shining lights in their eyes. Members of the Vichy Police and the Gestapo had been watching the area and when all was quiet they made their move, storming the building and taking the escapees by surprise.

They are herded into vehicles and driven to the local headquarters where they are locked up. For hours they are questioned, threatened and yelled at, yet the men remain silent. The captors, frustrated with their inability to make the men talk, try to call their superiors for advice but discover the phone is dead.

Suddenly, a group of heavily armed men storm the jail

and begin shooting. The escapees hit the floor as bullets fly over their heads. They have no idea who the men are. In moments, most of the Vichy Police and Gestapo lie dead or dying as the gunmen shoot open the jail doors and herd the captives out the back and into trucks. From there, they are reunited with the rest of the group and taken to the home of Madam Marguerite Avons and her son Serge. Serge is also a fugitive from the French police because of his resistance activities. In Switzerland, Serge had been active in obtaining false identities for escaping Allies. The authorities tracked him down and he narrowly escaped. He, too, is hoping to escape the country.

Originally, the stay was to be short. But with so many police dead and known escapees in the vicinity, heavy travel restrictions are in effect. The next move, set for Perpignan, is on standby for the next 28 days, until things cool down.

But things don't cool down. The Germans take over the transit and travel becomes even more dangerous than before. The group decides to risk it.

On February 2, 1944, each escapee is given forged papers and a guide who speaks both German and French. Their first hurdle is to get out of the area — which means crossing the Rhone River. The Germans have all the bridges under tight security but Serge, who grew up there, arranges for a small boat. The men cross at a pond downstream from the main road.

They are met on the other side by M. Blanc, who leads

the group to the train station where they split into groups of two to travel from Lyon to Perpignan. In addition to their guide and papers, each escapee is given a Colt .45 automatic pistol while on board the train. The train trip is uneventful, and they ditch the guns once they leave the car and rejoin their group; on the train the guns could help, on the street they would be a death sentence.

Fletcher can taste freedom as soon as they leave the train in Perpignan. The town is only about 55 kilometres from the Spanish border; once they cross into Spain, the rest of their journey will be easy.

Taking no chances with freedom so close, the group is divided once more; some stay at the Hotel Centre, the others in an apartment with Suzanne Dedeau, an English teacher at the nearby college. Before the war, she had been a French professor at Mt. Holyoke College in South Hadley, Massachusetts. Like all those helping the Allies escape, her life is in jeopardy. If caught, she would, at the very least, be tortured and held before being released. At the worst, she could be shot.

It takes five days before the connections can be made with their Spanish guide, Joseph Ferrusola, who takes them across the Pyrenees Mountains to Barcelona.

From Barcelona they drive to Madrid, then sail around Cadize into Gibraltar on a cargo ship. They fly to England and land safely on English soil February 25, 1944.

The Gestapo raided the Dupuis' farm after they left and

arrested the whole Dupuis family. All but Maurice are held for three weeks. Maurice is sent to a concentration camp where he is interned for months. Shortly after he is finally released, Maurice dies of malnutrition.

M. Blanc is also caught by the Gestapo while helping other airmen to escape. He is held and tortured for a month, then shot.

Suzanne Dedeau survives the war and meets the men she helped to escape. She passes away after a battle with cancer in 1956.

Chapter 9
Halifax LW682 — The Plane Called Mother

t's the afternoon of May 12, 1944, and the aircrew of No. 426 Squadron (Thunderbirds) knows that the big push is coming. All week they have been flying raids and they can feel the war building to a climax — it's only a question of when the final offensive will begin.

The first thing Flight Sergeant Wilbur B. Bentz does this morning, which is the first thing he does every morning here at Linton-on-Ouse in Yorkshire, England, is look at the notice board to see if there's a battle order posted.

There is, and they're on it. All it says, though, is that it will be a night mission.

His heart turns over. He stands and stares for a minute,

his stomach doing flip-flops, and he isn't sure if he's excited or scared. Perhaps he's both. There's a thrill about being a pilot, and he loves it, but dropping bombs on another country under threat of attack by enemy fighters brings up darker emotions.

The pilot, Wilbur (Wib) Bentz, is from North Bend, British Columbia. He's keenly aware that he and his crew are considered a green crew, and that most of the losses experienced in Bomber Command involve green crews. For some reason, the magic number is 15 operations (ops) when an aircrew is no longer considered green and their chances for survival improve. This mission will be Wib's third. And green or not, he's no stranger to the sick feeling in the pit of his stomach when a bomber doesn't return, and the guilt he feels at his own survival. How can people next to you die and you live? Who makes that decision and why?

He tries not to dwell on death. A friend of his once told him that those who go off to war knowing they could be killed live, while those who think it could never happen to them never return. Wib doesn't know if that's true or not, but he has no trouble believing that anytime he flies over enemy lines, he's got a good chance of never coming back.

The crew gathers silently around the notice board, each with his own thoughts. For Pilot Officer Joseph Arbour, an air-gunner from Montreal, Quebec, this will be his first ops, and Wilbur feels protective of him. Sergeant Roy Ellerslie is next to Joe, and everyone laughingly calls him RAF Roy. He's the flight engineer from Doncaster in Yorkshire. This will be mission number two for Roy.

Behind the pair stands Pilot Officer Jack McIntyre. As a wireless operator, he's got one of the safer jobs, not that any are really safe once you leave the ground. He's from Biggar, Saskatchewan, and the others tease him about being a farm boy. Standing on Wilbur's other side is Flying Officer Clifford Phillips, the bomb-aimer from Valparaiso, Saskatchewan. These two flat-landers have only flown ops once before.

Sergeant Fred Roach is next. A rear gunner, his position has the highest mortality rate of the aircrew, and the whole plane depends on him. He sees the enemy coming and gives the pilot evasive instructions. His guns are usually the first to encounter German fighters, and the first target of the enemy attacks. He hails from Leamington, Ontario, and this will be his third ops.

Sergeant Jack Summerhayes mans the mid-upper turret and is closely connected to the rear gunner. He covers his back — the area the rear gunner can't see. He'll be on mission number two. Jack stands quietly with a big smile on his face. His son was born a few months ago, and the smile is never far from his lips. He carries a picture of his boy in his front pocket wherever he goes.

Finally, Flying Officer Tom Taylor — the "old man" — is 29. This will also be his second mission. A native of Chisholm, Alberta, Tom likes to think of himself as a cowboy. He's the navigator, working closely with the pilot all through the flight. He likes to joke and say he's the only crew member brave enough to tell Wilbur where to go.

Wib considers his crew to be the best there is. He trusts all of them with his life and would lay down his own for each and every one of them.

They have no idea where they're going, what time they're leaving, or what the target will be. They'll find out the specifics at briefing time, only hours away.

The crew each go their separate ways, and Wib decides to take a short walk to relax. He looks to the southeast, toward the sea to the sky above Holland and Germany. The sky is pale, and the trees stand black and stark against the colours of sunrise. It's always a surprise to see nature unmindful of the war of men.

The target is Louvain, Belgium; the order of battle is 120 aircraft: 96 Halifaxes, 20 Lancasters, and four Mosquitoes, all from 6 and 8 Bomber Groups.

A light meal is laid out for those taking part in the night's ops; no one is ever sent out on a mission with an empty stomach, unless it's his choice. After their meal, they make their way to the barracks for their final rituals. Wib re-reads a letter he received from his sister, Romaine. She's always tried to mother him, and he's never been very good at letting her. Of all the people back home, he misses her the most.

The men carefully sort and shred their private papers and letters, and put their personal effects together with a note of how they want them to be dispersed if they don't make it back. When it's done, they feel empty, almost as if they've prepared for their own funerals.

The transport arrives late in the evening to take them to the hangars. The crew piles into the already crowded bus and silently bumps their way out to the fields where they finish getting kitted up. There are last minute changes, additional flight maps, and last minute briefs. When the group arrives at the hangar, some of the navigators are already working around a large table with topographical maps and plotting charts. It's all business, interrupted by nervous laughter and lame jokes. Stress is high and the tension in the air is almost tangible.

Geared with Mae Wests, parachute harnesses, and survival kits, the crews are ready to board the bombers. Each man grabs a helmet, tucks his bulky parachute under one arm, and tries to saunter outside casually to wait for the transport. Wib and his crew act nonchalant, as if they've been on 30 ops instead of being green. It doesn't work, and the other crews slap them on the back with comments about making sure they head in the right direction and don't mistake one of their own for the enemy.

The last hint of daylight is fading, leaving some objects overly bright, others in silhouette. Birds flock to roost in the trees, fighting over branches and chirping without a care in the world. A rabbit nibbles on some grass beside the hangars. In the distance a dog is barking. Everything is so peaceful, so normal, so far away from the war and the group of men leaving the earth on a mission of destruction. Some are flying off to their deaths, yet around them, the world continues as it has for a thousand years.

There's a slight chill in the air; it'll be a cold ride tonight. Wib draws his collar up around his neck. Jack smiles at him as he puts his son's picture back in his pocket. Roach stomps out the remains of one last cigarette.

Nearby, the padre hands out flying rations, and the doctor offers caffeine pills to anyone who wants them. Scrambling onto the trucks, they're packed in like sardines. The smell of sweat mingles with the dew-laden air, and the bus is silent as each man thinks his own thoughts.

Each crew member is dropped off at their dispersal point with shouts of "Give 'em hell," and "See you in the morning." No one wants to see an empty chair opposite them in the mess for breakfast, but chances are good there will be more than one man not coming home.

At the aircraft, Wilbur's crew stands patiently in the fading light until the flares take air, broadcasting the "stand by stations" command. Wilbur climbs into the cockpit of Halifax LW682, M for "Mother." He hangs his parachute on the hook behind his seat and straps himself in. Hooking up the gosport to the intercom, he cranks it up and puts on the headphones, makes sure the oxygen supply is working and then goes through his checklist.

"Mid-upper, all clear, Skipper," Jack Summerhays calls out over the intercom.

"Navigator, good to roll," Tom reports.

"Wireless, ready," says Jack McIntyre.

"Bomb-aimer, let's get on with it," Clifford chuckles.

"Flight engineer RAF Roy, ready when you are, Skipper."

"Rear-gunner, all set," Fred calls out.

The pilot gives the all-clear signal to the ground crew. *Thunk.* The chore-horse connector sockets into position, ready to supply the energy to turn over the four Rolls-Royce engines. The ground crew hooks up the booster battery assembly to each of them. Wilbur hits the switch, and engine one grunts and hiccups. The port propeller starts to slowly move, building up to a high-pitched whine, rumbling with unleashed power. As if reluctantly, a puff of smoke rises from the exhaust of number two engine as it fires, then three, and four, until the hunky metal bomber is purring.

The ground crew pulls out the chock blocks from under the wheels, and the airmen feel the plane hesitate before tentatively pulling forward out of the bay and out to the perimeter.

"Take us up, Mother," Wilbur says under his breath as she gathers speed on the perimeter.

The pilot takes a deep breath and relaxes a bit into his seat. Up to this point, the intercom has been alive with crew banter; nervousness played out in jests and laughter. It dies down as they wait impatiently for their turn on the runway. The bomber in front thunders down the tarmac with ground-shaking power and heads for the clouds.

Behind them, another heavy creeps to a stop, awaiting its turn.

As the plane ahead finds air, Wib pulls up to the line and reports to the tower that they're ready for takeoff. After a pause, the tower clears them to pull out, and the pilot tells the crew to assume their final takeoff positions. Bracing himself, he gets a firm grip on the control column. His heart is pounding in his throat, beating in tandem with the throb of Mother's engines.

Pumping the left rudder pedal followed by the right, he tests the stick for side-to-side movement. He checks the brakes, and then checks them again. Finally satisfied, he runs the engines to their upper limits and pulls the two throttle levers all the way back. The sound of the piston engines shifts from a teeth-clenching whine to a throaty rumble of pure muscle. Wib engages 30 degrees of flap for takeoff. The pilot stares at the flashing light on the side of the signal hut off the port wing. His stomach is in knots and he catches himself holding his breath while he waits. The flashing green light on the hut's windshield switches steady on and his heart catches in his throat. The Halifax lurches forward, pulled along the tarmac by the mighty engines. Instinctively, his body tenses in anticipation of the rattle, bang, and G-force rush as the beast gathers to leap.

All four engines build high, and Mother vibrates almost violently. Counteracting the torque, Wilbur pushes the throttles. The Halifax MKIII shudders to escape the earth and the back draft from the props rushes and swirls through the body of the plane. The roaring subsides minutely and the propellers find their rhythm with the rest of the bomber.

The pilot advances the throttles and nods for Roy, the engineer, to hold them steady while he focuses on the control column, gripping it firmly in both hands. Thundering forward, Mother strides for the air. The crew feel a slight fishtailing as a gust of wind catches the propellers. Wilbur is ready for it and corrects instantly, but not before stomachs flip. Faster and faster, the bomber rattles and bangs down the airstrip.

Mother reaches 160 kilometres per hour and, as the tail lifts off the ground, Wilbur feels the shift in his gut telling him to pull back on the controls. They leap upward, oddly weightless, thirsting to be free of the white streaks of light lining the airstrip. Rising against the wind, the plane climbs steadily into the blackness above, shifting up and down and side to side with the air currents. Darkness and cold envelop the men as the landing gear thumps into place. The vibrations ease and the crew relaxes. This is the best part of flying.

Slowly, the throttles are pulled back through the gate and fixed as they reach the course altitude of 5.5 kilometres above the earth.

Hours later, as they near enemy territory, the external lights are extinguished and night adds to the loneliness inside the black metal tube with its 6,000 kilograms of TNT rattling in the bombing bay. Below is the ocean, hidden from view by the clouds; ahead is the mainland, the target, the enemy, and death — death on the ground and in the air. Death is the known part of the equation, the unknown involves who and how.

So far, there has been no challenge to the Allied intrusion. Up ahead, the Pathfinders are marking the way with coloured flares, letting the enemy know the bombers are coming and lighting the way for them to find the target. The fighter escort is close behind and around the bombers, ready to defend them with their lives.

The swarm reaches the target area and starts to descend. Wib's aircrew can barely make out the shapes of a few Allied bombers; they are nothing more than mere grey glimmers of metallic shadows in the darkness. It's comforting to know they aren't alone. It makes them feel less vulnerable. And having the others so close helps to dispel the dreamlike quality of the continual throbbing of engines, the cold drafts through the plane, and the monotony of hours of night flying.

In minutes they're over the target of Louvain, and next in line for the dive to drop their load. The red flashes and puffs of smoke from flak fill the sky; searchlights brighter than daylight weave back and forth above and around them. Mother is flying into the worst of it, bucking and jumping. The pilot fights to keep her steady. All he wants is to drop their load and get the hell out. Planes are being hit, smoking engines fill the air with an acrid stench; whistles of badly damaged planes fill the ears. Below them bombs burst, throwing debris skyward. Above them are more planes, theirs and the enemy's. Dogfights twirl in and around the heavies, broken planes plummet to the earth, and parachutes dot the horizon.

Below them the ground is lit with lines of reconnaissance flares like candles on a Christmas tree. The tenacious bulldogs of the German Luftwaffe are not giving up as engines blow, planes explode, and airmen from both sides jump from crippled aircraft.

Clifford takes over the intercom, telling the navigator to flip the master switch and the pilot to open the bomb doors. The plane finishes the dive at 365 metres and releases the bombs, levelling just long enough for the camera to take the picture before pulling up, banking port, and heading for home. Flak is still exploding all around them, searchlights still hungrily scour the heavens for targets. Wib concentrates on breathing calmly and tries not to think farther than getting out of harm's way.

Wilbur's knuckles, suddenly white from tension, grip the column as he sits forward, straining to see what he's flying into. He feels the danger before the rear-gunner spots the night-fighter closing in.

Fred yells through the intercom: "Jerry coming at us from the bottom, Skipper, corkscrew starboard!" Wilbur jerks into action, and the bomber violently responds, twisting in ways planes were never meant to twist. All through the aircraft rivets ping and then pop. The men are thrown this way and that, and equipment smashes against the roof. Martin

Drewes, the German fighter pilot from III Gruppe, flying a Messerschmitt Bf110, squeezes off a couple of rounds, and a string of flaming beads flies into Mother's port engine. The plane jumps as the engine billows flames and black smoke. Mother is wounded, and following the lead of the searchlights coning the metal threat above them, anti-aircraft guns zero in on the limping bomber. Wilbur dives again, then climbs, continuing to twist and turn although his manoeuvrability is severely compromised with one engine down.

The crippled bomber is in trouble, and the pilot fights to keep her in the air. He orders the crew to prepare to bail out. Flames now stream out behind the blown engine as fuel leaks liberally into the air. Wilbur knows they're going down and is helpless to stop it. He knows they're somewhere over Belgium. The Halifax is spiralling out of control. They can't jump, and even if they could, he's seen what some night-fighters do to airmen helplessly suspended by parachutes. When he's finally able to level so the crew can jump, they've lost too much altitude. He can hear the wireless operator tapping out their location in code. Ahead is a marsh. With luck, they can belly land and make it out of the plane. It's their only hope. Wib takes a deep breath and prays for strength. He grabs the stick and fights to keep the bomber level with the ground, hoping the fuel doesn't ignite. The crew brace for the impact.

LW682, M for Mother, plummets to the ground, trailing flames and smoke, and the bog in Belgium rises up to greet it.

It hits, skids for a short distance with sparks flying from metal on rock, and then explodes. Debris shoots into the air, and along with it, five bodies from the crew of eight.

The five airmen's bodies thrown from the plane are recovered by the Germans and buried in Belgium. Three men are officially listed missing in action for 53 years: 21-year-old Pilot Officer Wilbur Bentz, 25-year-old Pilot Officer Fred Roach, and 23-year-old Pilot Officer Jack Summerhayes. Their bodies are never found.

Epilogue
The Relic Hunter
— 53 Years Later

The marsh smells like all marshes smell: fish, decaying mate-rial, and fresh water that has been frozen and warmed year after year. Mud sticks to the boots like the gumbo on any Saskatchewan field during spring thaw, and it's the mud that makes the task of raising up a 53-year-old Halifax out from under three metres of the stuff a miracle.

There had been talk of recovering the aircraft long before 1997. Three RCAF airmen were missing, and their families never knew for certain if they had died during the crash. The families always hoped that they were in a POW camp somewhere and had either been injured or, for whatever reason, were unable to tell anyone who they were. When the war ended, the hope lingered — for years. Families pored hungrily over pictures of POWs released after the war, in case their loved ones were among them. But the years wore on, and while their hope was tempered by logic, the weakness of broken hearts yearned for an answer or at least for closure. There was neither, and parents passed away not knowing the fate of their sons, children grew up without fathers, and nieces and nephews were born never knowing the uncle who was listed as MIA. There were no bodies, no graves, no ending. The next generation inherited not only the memories, but also the loss.

The challenge of draining the water from the bog and then digging through the sludge with heavy equipment on soft and unstable ground always seemed too daunting a task whenever the topic of raising the aircraft came up. There were 115 unsolved Canadian MIAs from World War II. Many felt that these three were at least solvable, if someone could only be passionate enough to get the job done. Someone passionate and able to raise the funds, to say nothing of dealing with the international issues of digging in someone else's country. The bog in question is in Belgium near Dender River.

The nephew of pilot Wilbur Bentz, Jay Hammond, found the right man in Karl Kjarsgaard. Jay's mother, Wilbur's sister Romaine, had passed away, and Jay had become determined to locate his uncle's aircraft and put an end to the family mystery. Jay, a fisheries biologist with the British Columbia government, contacted Frank Mergen, a Luxembourg national who was studying pharmacy at the University of Louvain. Frank had previously initiated the contact on a fisheries issue. Jay countered with an issue of his own, knowing the plane crashed somewhere in Belgium. What began as a chance communication turned into a long and close friendship. Frank was able to locate eyewitnesses to the crash and went to the site to see what the challenges would be in recovering the plane. That's when Jay found Karl.

Kjarsgaard, a middle-aged man of medium height with gray-blonde hair, was a pilot with Canadian Airlines International. He had already played a key role in the recovery of a Halifax from Lake Mjosa in Norway in 1995. That bomber, NA337, is now on display at the RCAF Memorial Museum in Trenton, Ontario. Karl took on this new project with his usual drive, and his enthusiasm was infectious. Once the funding and volunteers were in place, the dig began.

On August 29, 1997, Jay flew to Belgium with two of his sons. Stopping on the way for a four-day visit with Frank, the group then carried on to Geraardsbergen, and on September 5, met up with Karl, his son, and members of the Belgian Aviation History Association. At the site, they were greeted by 50 Belgian volunteers, including local fire, police, military, and forensic experts. The people of Belgium still think highly of the Canadians who fought for freedom in World War II, and all were excited to be part of this recovery.

The cheerful volunteers were a welcome sight for Karl and Jay. They drained the bog over a two-day period at the end of August. It sat that way for five days, but the mud was still damp and hard to work with.

The volunteers literally dug in, and the top of the plane was found under three metres of mud. After digging down to the bomber, they worked sensitively and very carefully to reveal the wreck. Finally after many hours, the remains of the three airmen were located and removed from the body of the aircraft named Mother, where they had been cradled for 53 years. Tenderly, and with passionate devotion, Karl laid a Canadian flag over our national war heroes. Slogging back to the shore through the mud, he retrieved his cell phone and dialled an Ontario number. Doug Summerhayes, the 53-year-old son of Sergeant Jack Summerhayes, had been waiting for the call. Karl, voice cracking with emotion and with tears rolling down his muddy cheeks, said:

"Doug, I found your Dad ..."

Karl Kjarsgaard is the father of three boys. As a parent, he loves each one them equally, even though they are very different. When Karl thinks of how fortunate his boys are to have their freedom and unlimited possibilities ahead of them, he truly appreciates what a wonderful gift they have been given. He appreciates that this gift came at a great cost: the sacrifices made by the young people of our military 60 years ago. He, for one, will never forget what those Canadians in World War II did for us. He has dedicated his life to making sure that future generations never forget what these Canadians fought and lost their lives for.

I asked Karl which of the three recoveries means more to him: NA337 from Lake Mjosa in Norway, recovering LW682 with the three airmen inside from Belgium, or his current project, the raising of LW170, 320 kilometres off the coast of Scotland. In his e-mail, I could picture an indulgent smile as he wrote his answer:

"Each plane is like one of my boys," he wrote. "Each one of them is unique, important, and close to my heart. They are the same."

His next rescue is of the LW170, depicted on the cover.

Bibliography

Achtung! Die Flugfestungen Kommen! Memoirs of WWII, by Lt. Col. John M. Carah, USAF (Ret.) 7th Edition — 1 Dec 2005.

A Doctor of Sorts, by V. J. Downie, 1992, published in Great Britain by Leo Cooper 1993.

Bonds of Wire, by Kingsley Brown, published by Harper Collins Toronto, 1989.

Chronicles of a Nervous Navigator, by John A. Iverach, published by Mrs. M. A. Peggy Iverach, 1997.

Fighter Squadron, by Larry Milberry, published by Canav Books, 2003.

Fourteen Days of Hell on an Ice Cap, Reader's Digest 1963, taken from MacLean's Magazine 1943.

Halifax, An Illustrated History of a Classic World War II

Bomber, by K. A. Merrick, published by Ian Allan Ltd, 1980.

No Moon Tonight, by Don Charlwood, published by Penguin Books Australia Ltd., 1987.

To Live Among Heroes, by George Armour Bell, published by Grub Street 2001.

Acknowledgments

Many of these stories seemed impossible to research. I came up against one dead end after another. Then, suddenly, I found a thread and when I followed it I discovered a bigger story than the one I had initially planned to write. The following is the list of all the amazing people who have helped me write this book. Without their help it would not be nearly as complete. I would like to thank each of the following:

Richard Goodlet, son of F/L David Harrison Goodlet, or "RCAF out in the Cold," at www.kwic.com/~pagodavista/dadstory.htm.

Laurie Abthorpe, Major Jay Nelles and wife Stacie, grandchildren of P/O Arthur Leroy Weaver, for "RCAF out in the Cold" and "From the Ice of the Arctic to the Heat of Battle."

Frank Haslam, for his help with "Escape." And thanks to Roy Brown, Michael LeBlanc, and the wonderful people at No. 207 Squadron RAF and the Royal Air Forces Escaping Society for "Escape."

Loraine Iverach, the daughter of the late John Iverach, navigator, RCAF. It's with her permission, pictures, and information that Dimi Havlicek's story was possible for "Czech Refugee Fights as a Proud Canadian."

Karl Kjarsgaard, at www.57rescueCanada.com, whose passion for the heroes of the RCAF has given back to Canada the Halifax. He helped in "Halifax LW682 — The Plane Called Mother" and "The Relic Hunter — 53 Years Later."

Michael McCabe, who donated his painting and prints to sell as a fundraiser for the next Halifax recovery and who kindly offered us the use of his print of LW170 for the cover of this book.

Warren B. Carah, who was kind enough to send me all kinds of material on Fletcher Taylor and the escape from Switzerland. He also sent me an excerpt from his father's memoirs; he was part of the escape party. Warren also gave me permission to use the information for this book in "Escape."

The text in the prologue has appeared variously in previous publications. It was first published in *Homemaker's Magazine* in 1999.

About the Author

Photograph: Blanshard Photography

Cynthia J. Faryon is an internationally published author and freelance writer. In addition to her World War II books, she has 19 travel reviews published as well as eight broadcasted travel pieces. Living in rural Manitoba, this mother of three enjoys a variety of interests including local history, music, and cooking. Her next project is a book on the legends and mysteries of WWI.

Photo Credits

Cover: painting by Michael McCabe; Cynthia J. Faryon's private collection: pages 46, 65, 76 (photographers unknown); Blanshard Photography: page 115; Royal Canadian Air Force Photographs: page 24 (photographer unknown).

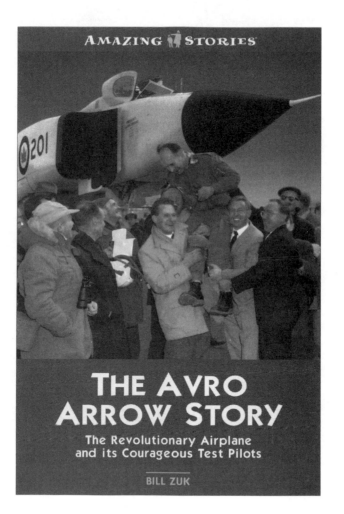

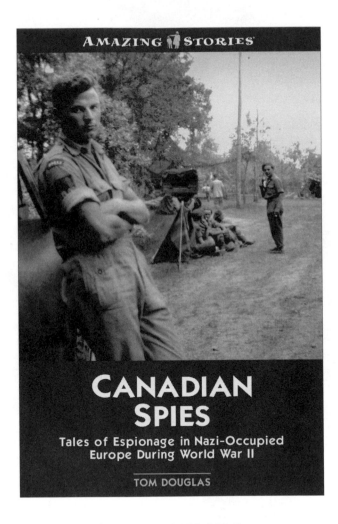

OTHER AMAZING STORIES®

These titles are available wherever you buy books. Visit our web site at **www.amazingstories.ca**

New **AMAZING STORIES®** titles are published every month.